J941 FULLER
Fuller, Barbara,
Great Britain /

CULTURES OF THE WORLD
Great Britain

Cavendish
Square
New York

Published in 2016 by Cavendish Square Publishing, LLC
243 5th Avenue, Suite 136, New York, NY 10016

Library of Congress Cataloging-in-Publication Data

Fuller, Barbara.
Great Britain / by Barbara Fuller and Debbie Nevins.
p. cm. — (Cultures of the world)
Includes index.
ISBN 978-1-50260-334-0 (hardcover) ISBN 978-1-50260-335-7 (ebook)
1. Great Britain — Juvenile literature. I. Fuller, Barbara, 1961-. II. Title.
DA27.5 F85 2016
941—d23

Writers, Barbara Fuller; Debbie Nevins, third edition
Editorial Director, third edition: David McNamara
Editor, third edition: Debbie Nevins
Art Director, third edition: Jeffrey Talbot
Designer, third edition: Jessica Nevins
Production Manager, third edition Jennifer Ryder-Talbot
Production Editor: Renni Johnson
Cover Picture Researcher: Stephanie Fletcha
Picture Researcher, third edition: Jessica Nevins

PRECEDING PAGE
The clock tower Big Ben is a symbol of London.

Printed in the United States of America

CONTENTS

GREAT BRITAIN TODAY

AFTER DOMINATING THE WORLD DURING THE NINETEENTH AND twentieth centuries, what will Great Britain do for an encore? Many centuries in the making, the British Empire by 1914 was the largest dominion in history, stretching around the globe and spreading English culture, language, and government to about one-fifth of the world's population. In terms of power and influence, Great Britain was great indeed. Not bad for a so-called "small island." But also, in the end, not entirely so good either.

Imperial Britain has been accused of causing many of the problems that are still festering in the world today: the domination of people of color and the subsequent harm to native cultures; the partitioning of the Ottoman Empire and the destabilizing of Arab lands in the Middle East—the clashes between India and Pakistan, and Israel and the Palestinians—the list goes on.

While the days of the Empire are mostly over, they cast long shadows a century later. Two world wars devastated the British nation, seriously diminishing its power. And one by one, British holdings declared, fought for, and won independence. The most recent example of this trend hit particularly close to home—in fact, right there

at home—when in 2014 Scotland sought independence from the United Kingdom (UK). Scotland was not merely a colony or other far-flung territory. Scotland, one of the three countries that make up Great Britain, was—and still is—an integral part of the UK itself.

The official response from the United Kingdom was telling. Prime Minister David Cameron made clear that the UK was not neutral on the question; it wanted Scotland to remain. However— and this is the point that proves how times have changed—the government said it would abide by the Scots' decision, as determined by popular vote. In the end, Scotland chose to remain a part of the UK, but the government's willingness

UK daily newspapers announcing the result of the Scottish independence referendum are displayed for sale in Glasgow, Sept. 19, 2014.

to arrive at a peaceful solution respecting the will of the Scottish people indicated a very new kind of Great Britain; a new vision of its greatness.

Another telling moment in the re-creation of Great Britain came in 2012 when London hosted the Summer Olympic Games. Already reeling from the 2008 worldwide economic recession, England was trudging through imposed austerity measures in an effort to reinvigorate its flailing economy. And yet at the same time, it needed to produce a grand global celebration with a stratospheric price tag, a commitment it had made prior to the economic meltdown. The previous Summer Olympics, in Beijing in 2008, were widely heralded as impossible to top. So what was the world's former head of the Empire but now diminished world power to do?

London is the only city in the United Kingdom to have ever hosted the Olympics, and it has done so on three occasions: in 1908, 1948, and 2012. For this latest one, it built a new sports complex, the Olympic Park, on a former industrial site in Stratford in East London. (After the Games were over, the

park was somewhat repurposed and renamed Queen Elizabeth II Olympic Park.) Some of the highlights of the London 2012 Olympics included these:

- Women's boxing was included for the first time as an Olympic event, and thirty-six women competed;
- Jamaica's track and field phenom Usain Bolt won a clean sweep of the gold medals in his races; and
- US swimmer Michael Phelps, competing in his third Olympics, won four gold and two silver medals, bringing his total Olympic medal tally to twenty. He set a new record as the most medaled Olympic athlete in history.

For many observers, however, the most memorable and distinctively British highlight of the Games was the Opening Ceremony. Host countries typically express pride in their country's history and culture through the Opening Ceremony. London embraced what is great about Britain and used it to present a quirky, affectionate, self-deprecating, but loving showcase of the best of the British people. And it was marvelous.

The Olympic flame burns in the cauldron during the Opening Ceremony of the London 2012 Olympic Games.

The four-hour production, "Isles of Wonder," was directed by Danny Boyle, a British film director, producer, and screenwriter. The spectacle told the story of Great Britain from ancient times to the present day through song, dance, and dazzling special effects. William Shakespeare, Harry Potter, Mary Poppins, The Beatles, James Bond, Peter Pan, Pink Floyd, and even Queen Elizabeth herself were just a few of the British cultural icons that made appearances throughout the show. The world's response to the production, which one critic deemed "a love song to Britain," was overwhelmingly positive.

The twenty-first century presents the British people with the challenge of deciding what the new Great Britain is going to be. What are its values? What is its place in the world? To be sure, the United Kingdom is still an economic and military power with considerable clout. It is one of the G8 nations, a group of the world's eight leading industrialized countries that meet regularly to discuss global issues.

For one thing, the "new" Great Britain is a far more diverse place than it used to be. The British people are increasingly made up of many races, ethnicities, and religions. The government has done much to accommodate this new reality, with a magnanimous spirit of tolerance and equality for all. This is partly the legacy of Empire, but also of increased immigration—Britain is a leading destination for immigrants because of its freedoms, relative prosperity, and safety.

British Prime Minister David Cameron (center), meets with Russian President Vladimir Putin (left) and US president Barack Obama at the 2013 G8 summit in Enniskillen, Northern Ireland.

As a result, Great Britain today is struggling with profound difficulties relating to multiculturalism and national identity. How can the country preserve its commitment to individual rights, a cornerstone of British values, with the influx of very different social, political, and religious values that have arrived with the multitude of immigrants? Terrorism—a menace the British lived with during the years of the Catholic versus Protestant "Troubles" in Northern Ireland in the second half of the twentieth century—has again raised its head in the form of Islamist radicalism. How does free speech jibe with certain Muslim clerics preaching hate and violence? A massive suicide bomb attack on London's transport network in 2005 signaled the depth of the threat and the critical nature of the problem.

British Prime Minister David Cameron gives a speech in 2014.

But time and again, Great Britain has proved its mettle. In 2013, after a spokesman for Russia's president Vladimir Putin publicly belittled Britain as being a "small island that no one listens to," UK Prime Minister David Cameron mounted a spirited defense.

"Let me be clear," Cameron said. "Britain may be a small island, but I would challenge anyone to find a country with a prouder history, a bigger heart, or greater resilience.

"Britain is an island that has helped to clear the European continent of fascism and was resolute in doing that throughout the Second World War. Britain is an island that helped to abolish slavery, that has invented most of the things worth inventing, including every sport currently played around the world, that still today is responsible for art, literature, and music that delights the entire world.

"We are very proud of everything we do as a small island—a small island that has the sixth-largest economy, the fourth best-funded military, some of the most effective diplomats, the proudest history, one of the best records for art and literature and contribution to philosophy and world civilization."

Welcome to Great Britain today!

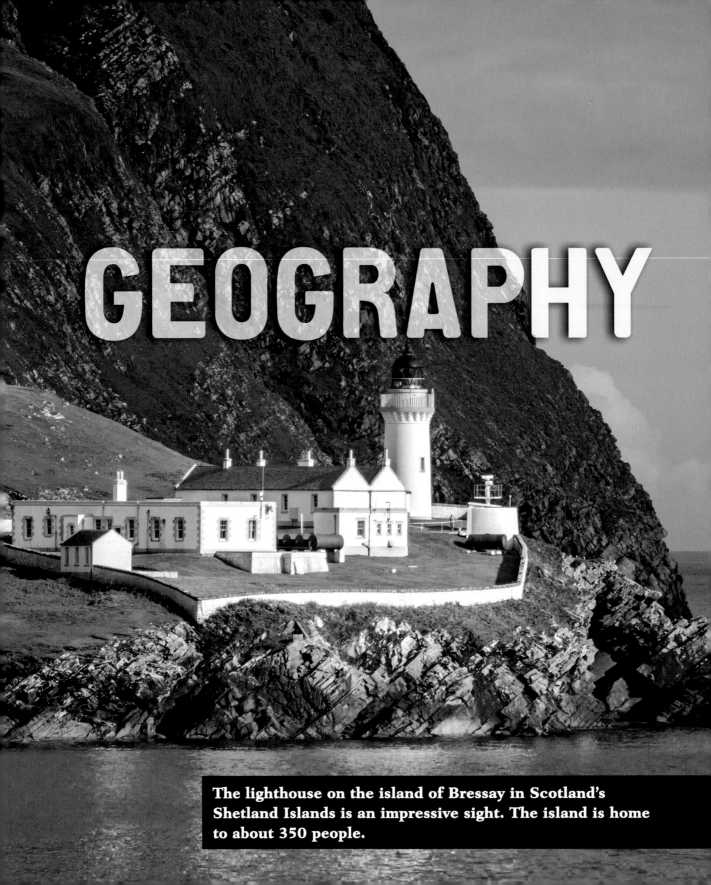

GEOGRAPHY

The lighthouse on the island of Bressay in Scotland's Shetland Islands is an impressive sight. The island is home to about 350 people.

THE EARLIEST KNOWN NAME FOR the island of Great Britain was Albion. We don't know what the people living there called it, because those earliest people left no written language. Albion derives from the Latin word *albus*, meaning "white," and dates to the writings of the Greek explorer Pytheas, who journeyed to northwestern Europe around 325 BCE. The name might refer to the impressive white cliffs on the island's south coast, the first view of the land for sailors approaching from continental Europe. Today the name Albion is still occasionally used in poetic or historical references.

When the Romans began their conquest of the region in 43 CE, they used the name *Britannia*, (derived from a similar name already in use there) to describe the southern part of the island. The northern part of the island (roughly today's Scotland) was *Caledonia*. The Celtic people living in Britannia were called Britons. (The Romans never fully conquered Caledonia.) Even after the Romans withdrew from Britain in the fifth century, when the Roman Empire collapsed, the name stuck. By then Britannia had taken on a symbolic female personification in the form of

The land that makes up Britain was once part of continental Europe. About eight thousand years ago, as the Ice Age ended, temperatures rose and the glacial ice cap melted. The waters flooded the vast continental plain of what are now the North Sea and the English Channel, creating the British Isles.

A statue of Britannia looks out over the city of Liverpool.

a Roman goddess also named Britannia. This goddess figure remains a symbol of British national identity to this day.

Britain took on the classification of "Great" Britain when, in the fifth and sixth centuries, large numbers of Celtic Britons migrated across the English Channel to northwestern France, bringing their language and culture with them. That area also came to be called Britannia, and the term *Britannia major* ("Greater Britain") distinguished the main island from *Britannia minor*, or "lesser Britain," (meaning, essentially, "farther-away Britain"). Today this region of France is called *Bretagne*, which is "Brittany" in English.

Great Britain is an island of three countries: England, Scotland, and Wales. It is located between 50° and 60° north latitude, and at 0° longitude. It is 600 miles (967 km) at its longest point from the north of Scotland to the southern coast of England, and 300 miles (483 km) at its widest point from the west of Wales to England's eastern coast. England is 50,350 square miles (130,410 square km) in area; Scotland is 30,420 square miles (78,790 square km); and Wales is 8,020 square miles (20,760 square km). Britain's total population is approximately 60.8 million, mostly concentrated in the southeast, particularly in the Greater London area.

Although Great Britain is separated from the European mainland, it remains connected geologically. That is, the main geological structures of Europe can be found in Britain: the great plain of northern Europe reappears as the windswept lowlands of eastern England, and north of these lowlands are remnants of Scandinavian mountains split by rift valleys. The fjords of Norway are repeated in the indented western Scottish coasts; ria (REE-ah) coasts (coastal inlets) like those of Spain and Brittany are found in South Wales; the German and Dutch estuaries and shores are echoed in eastern England, with submerged river mouths and wide shallow bays; and the white cliffs of Dover in Kent mirror those of Picardy in France, only 20 miles (32 km) away across the English Channel. Britain's highlands lie in the north and west, with a central belt of lowlands farther east.

THE MANY NAMES OF BRITAIN

Great Britain, Britain, England, United Kingdom—what's the difference? Do all these names describe the same place? The answer is yes and no. Although there is a quite a bit of overlap between them, there are differences based on the geographical and political definitions.

GREAT BRITAIN *is an island in the North Atlantic, the largest of the British Isles. It is also called Britain. It's the largest island in Europe and the ninth-largest island in the world. Britain is made up of the countries of England, Scotland, and Wales, and is surrounded by more than one thousand smaller islands. Politically, the term Great Britain refers to the combined countries of England, Scotland, and Wales, along with a number (but not all) of the surrounding islands. The term Great Britain does not include Northern Ireland, which is part of the United Kingdom, or the Republic of Ireland, which is an independent nation. Both Northern Ireland and the Republic of Ireland are located on the island of Ireland, which lies to the west of Great Britain.*

BRITAIN *is used interchangeably with the term Great Britain, and is sometimes used casually to refer to the United Kingdom as a whole. Others say it means only England and Wales.*

ENGLAND *is the largest and politically the most dominant country of Great Britain and the United Kingdom. The term England never refers to the whole of Britain; it is only one of its countries. On the other hand, the terms Britain or British are often used in reference to England or the English.*

UNITED KINGDOM, *also called the UK, is a political entity, not a geographical one. It is the union of the countries of England, Scotland, Wales, and Northern Ireland.*

UNITED KINGDOM

Buttermere Lake lies in England's Lake District.

ENGLAND

England has a variety of geographical regions:

NORTH WEST This region extends from Scotland to the north to Wales in the southwest. It lies on the coast of the Irish Sea to the west, and reaches east to the hilly Peak District, and south to the Midlands. It also includes England's famous Lake District.

THE PEAK DISTRICT This upland region in the north central part of the country became Britain's first national park in 1951. A horseshoe ring of sandstone ridge surrounds a limestone plateau with rivers flowing southeast, is bordered by Nottingham, Stoke-on-Trent, Greater Manchester, and Sheffield. Its wild moorlands and craggy rocks are popular with climbers and walkers. The Pennine Way footpath, which is 268 miles (431 km) long, starts here.

Northwest of the Peak District lies Lancashire; to its east over the Pennine Hills is Yorkshire. An age-old rivalry between the two counties, based on two families' claims to the English throne, dates from the fifteenth century.

THE LAKE DISTRICT In northwestern England, north of Lancashire, lies a mountainous area of radial hills interspersed with glaciated lake-filled troughs. Called the Lake District, or The Lakes, the 885-square-mile (2,292 sq km) region attracts tourists year-round. The country's highest mountains and deepest and longest lakes are found there, and all the land above 3,000 feet (914.4 m) in elevation is included in the National Park of England.

Lake Windermere, England's largest lake at 11.23 miles (18.08 km) long, is popular for pleasure cruises and boating activities. England's highest mountain, Scafell Pike, elevation 3,210 feet (978 m), attracts climbers; indeed, hiking is a favorite activity throughout this picturesque region.

NORTH EAST Bordering Scotland to the north, this northernmost region includes Northumberland, County Durham, Tyne and Wear, and North Yorkshire. Its coastline is on the North Sea. County Durham lies on a coalfield, with steel and other heavy industries in Consett. It is also traversed by the rugged moorlands of the Pennine Hills.

Within the county, the city of Durham is a medieval university town, surrounding a cathedral on a steep hill encircled by a river. Dating from 1093 CE, Durham Cathedral is a designated United Nations Educational, Scientific, and Cultural Organization (UNESCO) World Heritage Site. (The cathedral was featured in the Harry Potter films as the Hogwarts School of Witchcraft and Wizardry.)

Durham Cathedral in England, a fine example of Norman architecture, is a major tourist destination.

The white chalk cliffs of Dover

Newcastle-upon-Tyne, once an important shipbuilding port, is now a vibrant cultural city, epitomized by its Gateshead Millennium Bridge. To the north of Newcastle lies Northumbria, where Hadrian's Wall, completed in 128 CE, stretches for 73 miles (117 km) across England from Wallsend, Tyne and Wear, to Bowness-on-Solway. Sheep farming and forestry are the main forms of agriculture in the region.

EAST ANGLIA Norfolk, Suffolk, Cambridgeshire, and Essex make up Britain's eastern bulge, known as East Anglia. Rarely rising above 300 feet (91 m), this region is characterized by the flatness of the land. The drained fens and broken-down glacial deposits make fertile arable land. This region has the lowest annual rainfall in the country. Norwich and Cambridge are historic cities in the region.

SOUTH EAST The chalk ridges of Kent's North Downs and Sussex's South Downs run parallel in an east-west direction and are broken by north- or south-flowing streams. They face inward over the Weald, a concentric series of clay valleys and sandstone ridges. The Hampshire Basin is ringed by chalk hills. Coastal resort towns include Bognor Regis and Brighton. Canterbury in Kent is the location of Canterbury Cathedral, England's main Anglican church. Southeast of Canterbury is Dover, also in Kent, which faces France across the narrowest portion of the English Channel. It is a major port for ferry service to France. Dover is also the home of the famous White Cliffs of Dover, striking chalk cliffs that can be seen, on a clear day, from Calais, France.

GREATER LONDON The counties surrounding London in the south-eastern part of the country are informally called the Home Counties. They include Berkshire, Buckingham, Essex, Hertfordshire, Kent, Surrey, and Sussex. London's suburban sprawl stretches out toward more picturesque villages in this region. The Chiltern Hills rise to over 800 feet (244 m) and have colorful beech woods. The valley of the River Thames extends from the river's source in Gloucestershire through Henley-on-Thames to the royal castle at Windsor and beyond to London.

The Eden Project in Cornwall is series of connected greenhouses.

SOUTH WEST The south-western part of England is informally called the West Country. It reaches west to a point called Land's End in Cornwall, on the coast of the Atlantic. This land mass separates the Celtic Sea from the English Channel.

The monoliths of Stonehenge are a popular tourist attraction on the chalk downs of Salisbury Plain. Dorset's moody countryside of pastures and barren heaths is described in the novels of Thomas Hardy, while the limestone and fossils of Lulworth Cove on the coast are a geologist's dream. Devon's pretty coastal towns contrast with the classic granite moorlands of Exmoor and Dartmoor, which have rocky tors (pinnacles) and upland plateaus. The Cornish coast is more rugged than Devon's and is a popular tourist area. The Eden Project in Bodelva, a chain of interconnecting greenhouses containing plants from around the world, is a major tourist attraction in Cornwall.

On the northern edge of the Somerset Plain are the Mendip Hills, where Cheddar Gorge—famous for caving, rock climbing, and cheese production—is located. Gold-colored oolite stone makes for picturesque towns and villages in the Cotswolds, such as Burford and Oxford. Bath is an eighteenth-century spa town; its thermal baths date from Roman times.

THE MIDLANDS Divided into the regions of West Midlands and East Midlands, the low plateau in the center of the country was the site of much of

Warwick Castle, a medieval castle built in the eleventh century, is a major touristic attraction.

Britain's industrial development. The areas near the Nottingham and Leicester coalfields are known as the Black Country. The industrial heritage of the area has become an important tourist and educational attraction. Coventry was a center of the auto industry. Near Telford, the Ironbridge Gorge Museums have an interesting collection of industrial inventions.

Warwick Castle, dating from the fourteenth century, is one of England's most important and impressive medieval castles. Stratford-upon-Avon, Shakespeare's birthplace, boasts Tudor-style black-and-white buildings, as well as the renowned Royal Shakespeare Company's Swan Theatre.

SCOTLAND

Scotland's Southern Uplands encompass the border area and the southern region with undulating pastoral farming land. Farther north, the large cities of Edinburgh on the Firth of Forth on the eastern coast and Glasgow on the west are sited 45 miles (72 km) apart at Scotland's narrowest neck. These cities are in the Central Lowlands that reach up to the Sidlaw Hills and the Ochil Hills of Strathmore.

The Grampian Mountains form the division between the Lowlands and the Highlands in Scotland. Aberdeen is an important oil-processing town for the North Sea oil and gas fields. The islands of Jura and Islay, to the north of the Firth of Clyde, are renowned whiskey-producing areas; thick woollen knitwear comes from the nearby Isle of Arran. Cut into the Highland Plateau, large glens—bleak and almost barren valleys—often have cold lakes called lochs (LOKS). Loch Ness, stretching in a southwest direction through Glen

More from near Inverness on the eastern coast toward Fort Augustus, is reputed to harbor a prehistoric monster. Britain's highest mountain, the 4,406-foot (1,343-m) Ben Nevis, is near the lake.

To the north of Glen More lie the North West Highlands, where the population density drops to six persons per square mile (2.5 per square km). In the uplands many people are tenant farmers. On small farms of five to ten acres (two to four hectares), they grow oats and potatoes and keep chickens. Besides farming, knitwear and tweed manufacturing are the local industries, while salmon and trout fishing, grouse shooting, and deer hunting are lucrative tourist attractions as well as popular pastimes for residents.

Scotland has more than 790 offshore islands, of which approximately eighty-nine are permanently inhabited (though some by only one or two people!). Most of Scotland's islands are part of four main groupings: the Shetland Islands; the Orkney Islands; and the Inner and Outer Hebrides (HEB-reh-deez).

The old city of Lerwick, in Shetland, Scotland, with its characteristic granite houses, dates back four hundred years.

WALES

The principality of Wales is 135 miles (217 km) long and 35 miles (56 km) wide. The Black Mountains and the Brecon Beacons are rugged mountainous regions of South Wales, the latter rising to about 2,660 feet (811 m). The coast of Pembrokeshire is a national park, home to numerous seabirds. Cardiff and Swansea are major cities of South Wales.

Most of the uplands of Central Wales are drained by the River Wye. To the east, the Welsh plateau breaks up into the Welsh border hills, cut through by the Severn Valley.

North Wales is more agricultural than the south. Sheep farming is the most effective use of this area characterized by high and glaciated uplands. Mount Snowdon is 3,560 feet (1,085 m) high, accessible by mountain railway as well as by walking trails. Welsh knitwear and woven fabrics from the upland regions are renowned for their quality.

A steam train climbs Mount Snowdon in North Wales.

CAPITAL CITIES

Britain's cities act as regional and cultural centers, important places for business and tourism. There are sixty-four cities in Great Britain; fifty-one are in England, seven in Scotland, and six in Wales. Each of the three countries in Great Britain has its own capital.

LONDON England's capital city is a center of international trade and finance, tourism, retailing, media, and government services. The area known as the City of London is the financial center. Located within its square mile are the Bank of England, the Stock Exchange, Lloyd's of London (insurance underwriters), and the headquarters of major banks. To the east of this area lies the Tower of London; farther east is the East End, formerly a center of the textile industry. The financial area has now been expanded eastward into the Canary Wharf development in the Docklands, a highly sought-after office and residential location.

In contrast, the West End is the entertainment district. Many theaters are located near Piccadilly Circus and Shaftesbury Avenue; Leicester Square has numerous movie theaters; Oxford Street and nearby streets are shopping areas; and Covent Garden has a prestigious opera house and a flourishing handicrafts market.

The Houses of Parliament overlook the Thames in Westminster. A large clock tower commonly referred to as Big Ben (which is actually the name of the bell in the tower) rises on the north side of the building. Westminster Abbey, located across the street, was founded by King Edward the Confessor in 1065. Government offices and ministries are found in Whitehall, with the residences of the prime minister and the chancellor of the Exchequer on Downing Street. The Mall leads from Trafalgar Square to Buckingham Palace. The British Museum and University College London are in the Bloomsbury area between the West End and the City.

EDINBURGH Edinburgh Castle dominates the Scottish capital. It overlooks the Royal Mile, a street of beautiful sixteenth- and seventeenth-century townhouses that runs from the castle to the Palace of Holyroodhouse, the

The Edinburgh skyline is graced by the castle,

Queen's official Scottish residence. Edinburgh has three universities and a growing computer industry. Other industries include engineering, food processing, alcoholic beverages, tobacco, printing, and electrical goods. It is also a center for medicine, banking, insurance, tourism, and law, and acts as a marketplace for Scottish beef and salmon.

CARDIFF The capital city of Wales, known as *Caerdydd* in Welsh, used to be a major port for exporting coal and steel. While these heavy industries have declined, Cardiff is now a service center for financial, insurance, and banking institutions, home to the Welsh Assembly, and a center for food processing and light engineering. The Millennium Stadium is a British national arena that seats seventy-five thousand people for rugby and soccer competitions.

RIVERS

THE THAMES The River Thames (TEMZ) is the longest river in England and the second largest in the United Kingdom. It rises in the Cotswolds in Gloucestershire and flows to the North Sea at Tilbury 215 miles (346 km) to the

Tourists (bottom left) enjoy the view from a capsule of the London Eye, Europe's tallest Ferris wheel, on the South Bank of the River Thames.

east. It winds through picturesque scenery until it reaches London. The Thames is used for a variety of boating activities. Rowing competitions are regularly held on the river at Henley, Oxford, and Eton, while the annual Boat Race on the Thames in London between teams from Oxford and Cambridge universities is a major highlight.

London's position on the river makes it ideally suited as a port; the Thames below Tower Bridge is an extremely important waterway. Large container ships dock farther downriver at Tilbury since they cannot pass the Thames Flood Barrier, which was opened in 1984 to prevent the flooding of London by an unusually high tide. The Dartford Tunnel that runs beneath the Thames and the parallel overhead bridge complete London's orbital motorway called the M25.

The Severn Bridge connects England to Wales across the river.

THE SEVERN   The River Severn is the longest in the United Kingdom, flowing about 220 miles (354 km). It rises in North Wales and runs through the border country with Wales before reaching the Bristol Channel estuary. Its tidal range can be as much as 40 feet (12 m) during spring tides. The Severn Bridge over the river just north of Bristol is a major road link between England and Wales as well as an engineering triumph. Built in the 1960s, the bridge is 16,955 feet (5,168 m) long and spans 1,496 feet (456 m).

CLIMATE

Britain enjoys a cool to mild temperate climate with few extremes of temperature. The greatest variation in weather is in the southeast, but throughout Britain, temperatures rarely exceed 90 degrees Fahrenheit (32 degrees Celsius) in summer or fall below 14°F (-10°C) in winter.

The Gulf Stream, a warm ocean current that crosses the Atlantic Ocean, produces warmer winters in the west of the country so that in January

Wild ponies graze in the New Forest in Hampshire, England.

northwestern Scotland can be considerably warmer than southeastern England. Warm and wet westerly winds prevail, and since most upland areas are in the northern and western parts of the country, it is these regions that have the heaviest rainfall: over 60 inches (152 cm) annually, mainly in the fall and winter, compared with a national average of 40 inches (102 cm). Mild winters and high rainfall in the west make the region well suited for livestock farming. By contrast, the sunny summers and flatter land in the east are more suited for arable farming. Throughout Britain the weather is always unpredictable, and therefore always a subject for conversation.

FLORA AND FAUNA

Britain has a diverse range of flora and fauna, despite increasing urbanization. Ten national parks in England and Wales conserve different types of rural environments. The uplands boast heather-strewn grouse moors, brackens, and a spiny evergreen shrub known as gorse. Wild roses and hawthorns flourish in southern England, wild daffodils herald spring in Yorkshire and the Lake District, and bluebell woods flourish in the Home Counties. There are 150 different types of grass in the British Isles. The English oak is abundant in forests such as Savernake Forest in Wiltshire and Sherwood Forest in Nottinghamshire, beech woods are found in the Chilterns, and pine forests abound in Scotland.

Wild deer and ponies are found in Hampshire's New Forest; deer are found in some other woods, including areas of the West County and in the Scottish Highlands. Foxes, otters, bats, badgers, and field mice have adapted to the urban environment and are found throughout Britain. The red robin is a popular and territorial garden bird. Coastal areas and plowed arable land attract seagulls and hawks, while the larger birds of prey soar over highlands and even freeways in search of food. The peregrine falcon and the ptarmigan are found in the Scottish Highlands. Gray seals are common in underpopulated coastal areas. Brown trout and grayling are often found in rivers, while salmon and eel spend most of their lives at sea but return to spawn in rivers.

INTERNET LINKS

www.youtube.com/watch?v=rNu8XDBSn10
"The Difference Between the United Kingdom, Great Britain, and England Explained" is a tongue-in-cheek but very informative video explaining the intricate interconnections between Britain and other British places around the world.

www.englandforever.org
Information about England relevant to this chapter can be found in this site's following sections: "Regions," "Cities," "Attractions," and Geography."

www.lakedistrict.gov.uk
This website of the Lake District National Park has photos, videos, web cams, a timeline, and a wealth of information.

www.visitscotland.com/en-us/about/nature-geography
Visit Scotland is the site of Scotland's National Tourism Organisation; the section "Scotland's nature and geography" offers many photos and in-depth information.

www.wales.com/en/content/cms/English/About_Wales/Landscapes/Landscapes.aspx
Wales Cymru, "the official gateway to Wales," has many informative sections including this one about its geographical features.

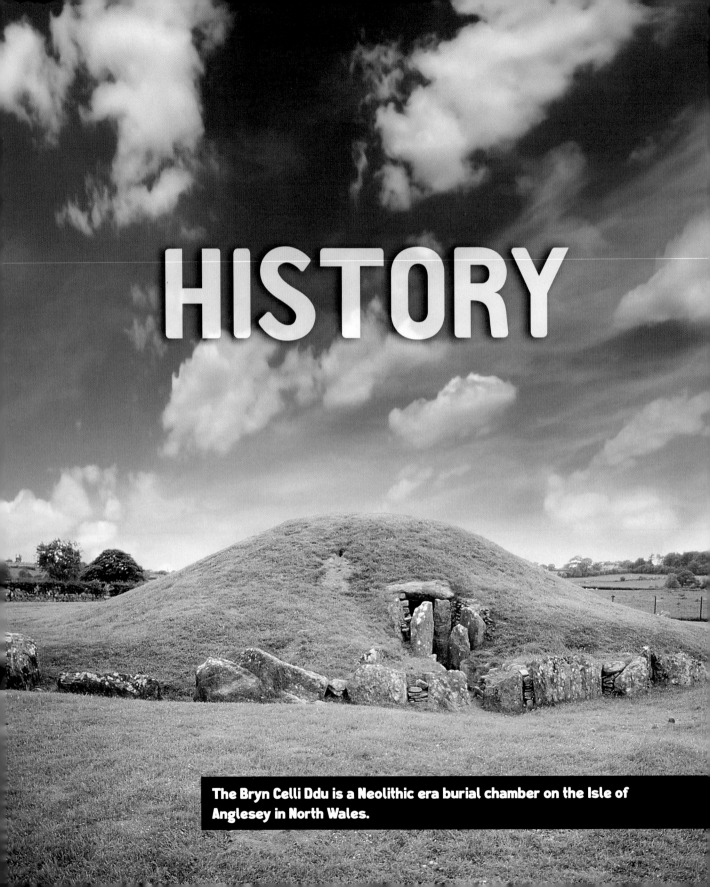

HISTORY

The Bryn Celli Ddu is a Neolithic era burial chamber on the Isle of Anglesey in North Wales.

THE HISTORY OF GREAT BRITAIN IS rich with countless stories. There are far too many events to relate here, and even the few that are mentioned are more complex and fascinating than can be relayed in such a quick overview. The kaleidoscope of years, places, and people—the details of their daily lives, their fears and passions, blood and battles, their ambitions and creations—have combined to make this unique place a mighty nation on a not-so-small island.

PREHISTORY

The history of people in Britain stretches back for more than nine thousand years. Archaeological evidence shows that Stone Age hunters and fishermen lived along the coast of western Scotland and on the islands of the Hebrides around 7000 BCE. Remnants of Britain's earliest Neolithic people, who arrived from the Iberian Peninsula and other parts of Western Europe around 3000 BCE, are seen in the barrows—the communal burial grounds on the chalk uplands of southern England. The Beaker People (so called because of their pottery skills) built hill forts,

STONEHENGE

By far the most famous of the mysterious ancient monuments found throughout Britain is Stonehenge. Located in Wiltshire, England, it is a circle of bluestones—huge stone monoliths—each weighing between two and four tons (1.8 and 3.6 metric tons). Some scholars believe the site might have once had eighty such stones, but only forty-three remain. The stones most likely came from Wales, some 250 miles away, raising the question of how they were transported such a distance in those days before the wheel.

The site might have been used as an astronomical observatory, a sort of primitive computer for calculating the dates of celestial events; or for spiritual rituals; or for ancestor worship—there are many burial sites nearby—or possibly as a place of healing. Perhaps Stonehenge had many functions over the millennia.

Britons in times past were just as mystified by Stonehenge as we are today. In fact, the strange monument appears in the King Arthur stories, dating from the early twelfth century CE. Today, Stonehenge is an iconic symbol of Britain, a UNESCO World Heritage site, and a top tourist attraction.

cultivated barley, and were buried in individual graves from around 2400 BCE.

Ritual landscapes called henges, some with standing stones and stone circles, can be found across all of Britain. Henges are earth-worked landscapes, usually circular, banked enclosures with a ditch. No one is certain what the purpose of these prehistoric landscapes was, but it's curious that they are found throughout Britain but nowhere else. Among the most impressive are the Ring of Brodgar in Orkney, Scotland; the Callanish Stone Circle on the Isle of Lewis, in Scotland; and the Great Circle at Stanton Drew in England, all built sometime between 3000 and 2000 BCE.

Around 700 BCE, different tribes of Celts arrived from Central Europe, bringing with them the knowledge of ironworking that revolutionized agriculture. They established hill forts and trade outlets on the River Thames and Firth of Forth. Their society was stratified and included a caste of Druid priests and a ruling warrior class.

CLASSICAL ERA The Romans invaded Britain in 43 CE and occupied the south of Britain from the Humber to the Severn rivers. They established garrison towns and brought Christianity to Britain. The Romans failed to

A section of Hadrian's Wall still remains after two thousand years.

conquer Caledonia (now Scotland), so the Roman Emperor Hadrian (reigned 117—138 CE) built a wall from coast to coast in the north of England to prevent incursions of Picts and Scots across the border. Hadrian's Wall, begun in 122 CE, was 73 miles (117.5 m) long, and from 10 to 20 feet (3 to 6 m) high. A large portion of still exists today; it is a World Heritage site and a popular tourist destination. Britain was part of the huge Roman Empire until its collapse, and the last Roman troops left the island around 410 CE.

MEDIEVAL BRITAIN

THE ANGLO-SAXONS Three Germanic tribes from regions that are now in Germany and Denmark invaded soon after the Romans left. The Angles settled in the east, the Saxons farther west and in the northern Midlands, and the Jutes in Kent and the South Coast. This drove the Celts farther north and west. The Anglo-Saxons founded the different kingdoms of Essex, Sussex, Wessex, Middlesex, East Anglia, Northumbria, and Mercia. Anglo-Saxon kings included King Offa of Mercia (reign 757—796), who built a long dike on the Welsh borders to keep the Celts at bay, and King Alfred of Wessex (Alfred the Great, 871—899), who enlisted educated churchmen to draw up laws. It was also in Alfred's reign that the *Anglo-Saxon Chronicle*, an extensive record of Britain's early history, was first written. Monks from the Scottish island of Iona and the Northumbrian island of Lindisfarne continued to spread the

English history is usually classified according to the following categories:

Anglo Saxon	c. 500–1066
Norman	1066–1154
Plantagenet	1154–1485
Tudor	1485–1603
Elizabethan	1558–1603
Stuart	1603–1714
Jacobean	1603–1625
Caroline	1625–1649
Interregnum ("between kings")	649–1660
Restoration	1660–1688
Georgian	1714–1837
Victorian	1837–1901
Edwardian	1901–1914
World War I	1914–1918
Interbellum ("between the wars")	1918–1939
World War II	1939–1945
Postwar	1945–present

Christian religion. In the late sixth century, the monk Augustine became Britain's first Archbishop of Canterbury.

Meanwhile, in 843 the Highland tribes of Picts and Scots were united into one kingdom under King Kenneth MacAlpin. The Lowlands of Scotland were inhabited by Britons and Angles from Northumbria. Wales was mostly settled by Celts by the eighth century, when family groupings became small kingdoms.

The Anglo-Saxons developed communal strip farming using large plows. A council of wise men—the Witan—issued laws and chose kings. In 865, Vikings from Norway and Denmark conquered and then settled in most of England.

THE NORMAN INVASION The last great Saxon king, King Edward the Confessor, who reigned from 1042 to 1066, allegedly promised the English throne to Duke William of Normandy. Normandy was a duchy (territory of a duke or duchess) in northern France that had been settled in earlier centuries by invading Vikings (the *Norse*, or "Northmen"). These Norsemen intermarried with the local people and came to be known as Normans. But when Edward died, Harold Godwinson of Wessex became king instead. In 1066 Duke William invaded the south of Britain and defeated and killed Harold in the Battle of Hastings and claimed the English throne.

King William I, known as William the Conqueror, saw England as his personal property. He deprived most Saxon lords of their lands and gave half to Norman nobles, one quarter to the Church, and kept most of what remained for himself. *The Domesday Book* of 1086 records landholdings and agricultural practices after William's land redistribution, and is today housed in the National Archives in London.

The history of Britain from this point forward is marked by the names of the succeeding royal houses, or dynasties: the Normans, the Plantagenets, the Tudors, and others.

THE PLANTAGENETS William's death in 1087 was followed by disputes over the throne. The infamous murder of the archbishop Thomas Becket in Canterbury Cathedral in 1170 was the result of a church-state dispute during the reign of Henry II (1154—1189), the first king of England from the House of Plantagenet. The Plantagenets were a family originally from the French province of Anjou. This house, or dynasty, would produce a line of fourteen English kings.

Of these, Richard I (1189—1199), known as Richard the Lionheart, went on several crusades to the Holy Land. His brother, King John, ruled so badly that the nobles forced him to sign the Magna Carta ("Great Charter") in 1215. The document guaranteed many political rights and personal liberties in Britain. During the reign of Henry III (1216—1272), nobles led by Simon de Montfort formed a council that became the Parliament. Edward I (1272—1307) conquered Wales, killing the Welsh leader Llewelyn

In 1485, King Richard III of England died quite horribly in battle at the hands of a Welshman. He was buried without fanfare in Greyfriars Church in Leicester, England. Over time, the church was demolished and the king's grave lost to legend. In 2012, however, archaeologists discovered the long-lost king's remains under a modern-day parking lot.

in 1282 and installing his own son, Edward II, as Prince of Wales in Caernarvon Castle in 1284. He also installed his own nominee on the throne of Scotland, but Edward II was defeated by the Scots at the Battle of Bannockburn in 1314 and Scotland remained independent.

Further royal disputes occurred in the late fourteenth and early fifteenth centuries. Edward II (1307—1327) was deposed and murdered. Under Edward III (1327—1377), England fought the Hundred Years' War with France, which lasted from 1337 to 1453 and resulted in England losing almost all of its French lands. This period was also marked by the Black Death, a form of plague that killed between 30 and 40 percent of Britain's entire population in just two years, from 1348 and 1350.

Under Henry VI (1422—1461), the nobles divided themselves into the houses of Lancaster and York in the Wars of the Roses. When Edward IV (1461—1483) died, Richard of Gloucester imprisoned Edward's sons in the Tower of London, where they were murdered, and then declared himself Richard III (1483—1485). The end of Richard III's reign in 1485 typically marks the end of the Medieval Era, or Middle Ages, and the start of the Early Modern period in England.

This is an example of the type of helmet a medieval knight might wear in battle.

REFORMATION, RESTORATION, REVOLUTION

The sixteenth, seventeenth, and eighteenth centuries saw many major events in British history. These include the English Reformation, the Scottish Reformation, the English Civil War, the Restoration of Charles II, the Glorious Revolution, the Treaty of Union, the Scottish Enlightenment, and the first British Empire.

THE TUDORS Struggles for the throne continued as various royal houses competed. Henry Tudor of Wales defeated Richard III in 1485 to become Henry VII (1485—1509). Although he was of the House of Lancaster, he married

During the Middle Ages, Christians throughout Europe went on religious pilgrimages. Groups of faithful would travel to a shrine or church to pray, seek divine forgiveness, and refresh their souls. The top destination churches, including the British cathedrals at Glastonbury, Canterbury, and Winchester, housed sacred relics—such as the purported bone of a saint, for example—as objects of veneration. These holy objects were thought to sanctify their surroundings and function as intermediaries for those seeking the protection and help of that particular dead saint.

Canterbury Cathedral

Another sort of pilgrimage was militaristic in nature. Thousands of faithful warriors would march off from various places in Europe to the Middle East to fight those they viewed as enemies of Christianity: Muslims, Jews, or even the Eastern Catholic Church. Sanctioned by the pope in Rome, the intent of these missions was to "take back" the Holy Lands and to bring them and other Mediterranean lands under the control of the Roman Catholic Church. From 1095 to 1291, a series of these Crusades took place, with the British taking part in some but not all of them. The romantic ideal of courageous knights in armor carrying the cross to defeat "the infidels" stems from this period. Participating in a Crusade was thought to be a way to achieve glory and certain admittance to Heaven. But in truth, the Crusades were bloody, vicious battles that were ultimately disastrous.

THE BLACK DEATH

Between 1346 and 1350, a plague killed 20 million people throughout Europe—about one-third of Europe's population. People called it the Black Death for the painful black swellings it produced on the skin, but they did not know what caused it. Terrified, they blamed everything from the wrath of God to astrology to swamp vapors. Many thought it signaled the biblical Apocalypse, or the end of time.

The plague reached Britain in the summer of 1348. The disease spread with lightning speed, sometimes wiping out entire villages, creating ghost towns with crops rotting in the fields and livestock starving. The plague had a devastating effect on the economy, society, and the entire culture.

Today, most scientists believe the disease was bubonic plague, spread by fleas that had bitten rats, though there are other theories. Over the next few centuries, the Black Death reappeared several times in Britain, in somewhat smaller outbreaks, and didn't fully subside until the late seventeenth century.

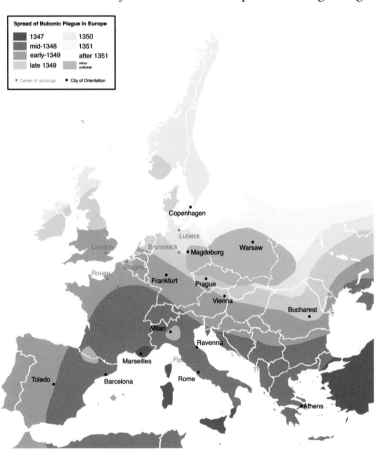

Spread of Bubonic Plague in Europe

1347
mid-1348
early-1349
late 1349
1350
1351
after 1351
minor outbreak

● Center of uprisings   ● City of Orientation

Elizabeth of York to end the feud. He pacified the powerful Welsh nobles and brought them under his control, and he tried to make the English crown financially independent.

His son, Henry VIII (r. 1509—1547), presided over a particularly scandalous reign, and became one of the most famous king's in Britain's history. The story of Henry VIII continues to fascinate people to this day. In his effort to produce a male heir to the throne, Henry married six times, executing two of his wives along the way. He tried to annul, or undo, his marriage to his first wife, Catherine of Aragon (who had become too old to bear children), so he could marry the young and reputedly beautiful Anne Boleyn. This attempt brought Henry into direct opposition with the papal authority in Rome, who refused to grant the king an annulment. In 1533 Henry split away from the Roman Catholic Church, establishing the Anglican Church with himself as its Supreme Head.

This portrait of King Henry VIII, dated 1540, is a famous painting by Hans Holbein "the Younger."

That prompted the English Reformation, or conversion to Protestantism. No longer needing the pope's permission, Henry married the now pregnant Anne. Like Catherine before her, Anne bore him a daughter but no sons, and eventually Henry wanted to get rid of her, too. He had her arrested on trumped-up charges; she was tried and ultimately beheaded, and Henry moved on to his next wife, Jane Seymour. Seymour did bear a son, but she herself died days later. None of Henry's remaining wives produced an heir.

On the political front, Henry brought Wales into legal union with England, and also declared himself King of Ireland.

As it turned out, all three of Henry's children would succeed him on the throne, his son Edward VI (r. 1547—1553); then his estranged daughter by his first wife, Mary I (r. 1553—58), who brought the crown (and therefore the country) back to Roman Catholicism; and finally his daughter by Anne Boleyn, Elizabeth I (r. 1558—1603), who reverted the throne to Protestantism once again and the Anglican Church has remained the official church of England ever since.

During Elizabeth's reign, considered one of Britain's most glorious, the Spanish Armada was defeated, English colonies were established in America, and education and the arts flourished. Elizabeth I, the last Tudor monarch, never married so the throne passed to her Scottish cousin James of the Stuart dynasty. He became James I of England (r. 1603—1625). His accession cemented the two countries together, although this was only finalized a century later with the Act of Union of 1707. Under James, the Authorized Version of the Bible was published in 1611, and the *Mayflower* set off from Plymouth, England in 1620 to found a new Puritan colony in America.

CIVIL WAR AND THE RESTORATION Conflicts between the Stuart kings—James I and his son Charles I (r. 1625—1649)—and Parliament would color the next several decades. In 1642, these conflicts led to a civil war between Royalists and Parliamentarians that lasted until 1645, when the Royalists were defeated at the Battle of Naseby. In 1649, Charles I and his

This painting depicts the Battle of Naseby, a turning point in the English Civil War.

wife were executed, and England became a Commonwealth under Oliver Cromwell until his death in 1658. Sporadic fighting continued against the Royalists.

By 1660, with no clear sign of a new leader, Charles II (r. 1660–1685), son of the executed monarch, was asked to return from exile to the throne. This period is called the Restoration. The Test Act of 1673 precluded any Catholic from holding public office. Charles II was careful to be accommodating in his reign, but his brother James II (r. 1685–1688) tried to overturn anti-Catholic legislation, married a Catholic, and was believed by many to be a Catholic himself.

THE GLORIOUS REVOLUTION Fearing that Catholicism had seized control of the monarchy, Parliament invited the Dutch king William, who was married to Charles II's daughter Mary, to invade in the name of Protestantism. He did this in 1688 in what became known as the Glorious Revolution. James II fled to France. William (r. 1688–1702) and Mary (r. 1688–1694) were offered the crown jointly by Parliament. From that time on, Parliament was stronger than the crown in Britain. In 1689 it passed a Bill of Rights which guaranteed individual liberties including the freedom of religion. In 1701 an Act of Settlement was adopted that allowed only a Protestant to inherit the crown, a law still in force today.

A portrait of Queen Mary II, who ruled in tandem with her Dutch husband King William

In 1707, the Act of Union united the kingdoms of England and Scotland and transferred the seat of the government to London. With it went many of Edinburgh's prosperous ruling class, leaving the Scottish capital in economic stagnation and aggravating other problems that would create social instability for years.

By 1714 Britain was the leading international power. It had colonies on the eastern coast of America, sugar-producing islands in the West Indies, a flourishing slave trade between Africa and America, and expanding trading interests in India, the Far East, and the Pacific. Economic life expanded. New canals and waterways improved the distribution of goods, and weekly

THE GREAT FIRE OF LONDON

One Saturday night in September 1666, a fire started at the house of King Charles II's baker, Thomas Farynor, who lived on Pudding Lane. Fires were not unusual in the crowded city, with most buildings being framed with timber. But it had been a hot, dry summer, and water reserves were low. As the fire spread, the news was reported to the mayor, Sir Thomas Bloodworth, but he remained unconcerned.

By the next day, with the fire growing still larger, the king was notified and he ordered the mayor to take action. Citizens rushed to destroy houses in an attempt to create firebreaks, but the response was too little, too late. The fire raged and spread and Londoners panicked. Thousands tried to evacuate the city, creating traffic jams in the narrow streets, while others looted the empty shops and houses.

The fire burned for more than four days, and in the end destroyed 373 acres (151 hectares) of the city. About 13,200 houses and eighty-four churches were lost, including St. Paul's Cathedral. The official death toll was a mere four people, but the true number was undoubtedly much higher. Some one hundred thousand people were left homeless.

As if the fire itself were not a sufficient tragedy, the aftermath saw a frenzy of accusations aimed particularly at foreigners and Catholics. Eventually, the blame was pinned on a mentally unstable man who was hanged for the alleged crime. But for the next 150 years, Londoners were all too willing to lay the real blame at the feet of the "Papists," or Catholics.

This painting (artist unknown) of the Great Fire of London is on display in the Yale Center for British Art in New Haven, CT.

markets were replaced by regularly stocked shops. And then the Industrial Revolution began in Great Britain and spread to Western Europe and the United States, creating new manufacturing and production processes and technologies—and the Modern Era began.

SUPERPOWER

In the eighteenth and early nineteenth centuries, Britain enjoyed significant victories in major wars. It was victorious in its war with France (1756—1763), and as a result, France lost all its territories in North America. Although Britain lost in its colonies in the American Revolution (1776—1783), Britain's victory over France in the Napoleonic Wars (1793—1815) earned it twenty new colonies. By 1820 Britain had colonized a quarter of the world's population, cementing its power and reputation.

This portrait of Queen Victoria with the Princess Royal Victoria in 1844 is the earliest known photo of the queen.

VICTORIAN AGE Queen Victoria (r. 1837—1901) presided over a golden age of British expansion, imperialism, and world domination. The two-party system in Parliament evolved in the 1860s, as Benjamin Disraeli and William Gladstone alternated as prime ministers and heads of the Conservative and Liberal governments respectively.

Overseas trade led to many foreign entanglements: in 1839, the start of the Opium Wars with China; in 1854, the Crimean War against the Russians; and in 1857, the Indian Mutiny, which briefly cast doubts on the colonial philosophy. Suez in Egypt was invaded in 1882 to protect Britain's shipping route to India. The Boer War (1899—1902) took place in South Africa amidst growing competition with other European powers for African colonies.

WORLD WAR I The reign of King Edward VII (r. 1902—1910) was overshadowed by a growing European military buildup and the onset of World War I in 1914. When Germany invaded Belgium, the British cabinet agreed that Britain must fight such aggression. British soldiers marched off to war with

Winston Churchill flashes the "V for Victory!" sign, a rallying cry for World War II Allies.

enthusiasm, but ended up enduring unspeakably horrible conditions while living in the trenches that bordered the battlefields. More than one million British soldiers died during the four years of "The Great War," but Germany was defeated. Britain, the United States, and France crafted the Treaty of Versailles, a peace settlement that imposed harsh conditions on Germany.

During the war, with the men away fighting, women worked in armaments factories and agriculture. At the end of the war in 1918, British women over the age of thirty gained the right to vote for the first time. During the 1920s, Britain experienced a severe economic depression and high unemployment. The world economic crisis hit Britain hard during the 1930s, with the industrial heartlands of South Wales, the Midlands, and the north of England particularly affected. From 1937 onward, the armaments industry revived as Britain prepared for yet another war.

WORLD WAR II The terms of the WWI peace treaty proved humiliating and economically disastrous to Germany, and by 1939, another global war heated up. Once again, Germany was the aggressor and this time it conquered most of Western Europe in less than two months. But under Prime Minister Winston Churchill, Great Britain resisted. WWII was devastating to Britain, as it was to many nations. In the summer and fall of 1940 the German Air Force waged an air campaign against Britain's Royal Air Force that came to be called the Battle of Britain. Beginning on September 7, the Germans bombed London for fifty-seven consecutive nights. Other cities across the United Kingdom were also hit. In the end, Britain prevailed, but at great cost in military and civilian lives, property destruction, and economic hardship.

POSTWAR In the 1940s and 1950s, there were food shortages and rationing in Britain, as well as large-scale reconstruction. Social measures passed

THE BRITISH EMPIRE

Britain began acquiring overseas possessions between the sixteenth and eighteenth centuries. At its height in the twentieth century, the British Empire was the largest empire in history—affecting one-fifth of the world's population. The British dominions, colonies, protectorates, mandates, and territories made up "the empire on which the sun never sets." The phrase meant the sun was always shining on one of Britain's holdings. However, it also implied that the sun would never set on the Empire itself; it would last forever. That would not be the case. During the second half of the twentieth century, many of Britain's colonies gained their independence.

Today, the era of Britain imperialism is essentially over. The United Kingdom retains sovereignty over fourteen small territories beyond the British Isles. Many of its former colonies and protectorates are among the fifty-three member states of the Commonwealth of Nations, an equality-based, non-political, voluntary association of countries. Sixteen Commonwealth nations share the British monarch as their nominal head of state.

The Empire's legacy includes the widespread use of the English language around the world. British culture, sports, and the parliamentary system of government have taken root in many of the former colonies. However, British imperialism is also blamed for causing disruption to the native cultures and social systems of those nations, causing the migrations of millions of people, and sowing the seeds of conflicts that continue today.

during these years form the basis of the existing welfare system. In 1952, King George VI died and his daughter Elizabeth began her reign as Queen Elizabeth II.

In 1973 the United Kingdom joined the European Community, which is now called the European Union (EU). It is a community of twenty-eight nations bound together by common policies in trade, environment, agriculture, and education. These policies are created by EU governing institutions. As part of the community, Britain has had to adopt EU laws and regulations on many areas of British society, including labor laws, human rights, racial discrimination, and the environment.

The United Kingdom joined the European Union (EU) in 1973.

TWENTY-FIRST CENTURY

After the September 11, 2001, attacks against the United States, in which sixty-seven British citizens died, the British government turned its attention to the problem of global terrorism. Prime Minister Tony Blair worked closely with the United States and sent troops into Afghanistan to fight al Qaeda, the organization responsible for the attacks. British troops also went to Iraq the following year, despite significant opposition from British officials and citizens, to oust Iraqi leader Saddam Hussein.

On July 7, 2005, Britain suffered a major terrorist attack of its own. A series of coordinated suicide bombings in central London killed fifty-two people and injured 700 others. The perpetrators were four British Muslim men—militant extremists—who died in the attack. The purported reason for the attacks was anger at Britain's foreign policies pertaining to the Muslim world. Following these attacks and other attempts, the British government has had to focus on developing new strategies for national defense and security as terrorism looms as a major threat in the twenty-first century.

In uncertain times, Great Britain's sense of identity has nevertheless remained solid and secure. In 2013, the widely beloved Queen Elizabeth celebrated her Diamond Jubilee, her sixtieth anniversary on the throne. That same year, the queen welcomed the birth of her first great-grandchild, Prince George of Cambridge, England's future king if all goes according to plan. And in 2014, Scotland voted to remain part of the United Kingdom and not declare independence, a decision that leaves the UK intact for now.

Explosions around London on July 7, 2005, brought a heightened awareness of terrorism to Great Britain.

INTERNET LINKS

www.historylearningsite.co.uk/england_medieval.htm
This British history site has a wide selection of topics relating to life in medieval England.

www.english-heritage.org.uk/discover/explore
The site English Heritage presents an excellent interactive history section.

www.royal.gov.uk/hmthequeen/hmthequeen.aspx
The official website of the British monarchy presents a section devoted to Her Majesty the Queen.

GOVERNMENT

Queen Elizabeth II has been Head of State of the UK since 1952. She became Queen at the age of twenty-five.

3

THE GOVERNMENT OF GREAT Britain is the government of the United Kingdom, which includes England, Scotland, Wales, and Northern Ireland. It is a constitutional monarchy. The monarch is the head of state, and has a predominantly ceremonial role, with duties that include the formal appointment of the prime minister, accepting the resignations of prime ministers before elections, and opening Parliament each year. The monarch also meets the prime minister weekly to discuss current issues and receives and entertains foreign heads of state.

NATIONAL GOVERNMENT

The UK government is a parliamentary democracy; elections are held at least every five years, and all citizens over the age of eighteen can vote. Generally, the political party that wins the most seats in Parliament leads the government.

Queen Elizabeth II is the fortieth monarch since William the Conqueror to wear the crown of England, now the crown of the United Kingdom.

PRIME MINISTER The prime minister is the head of government in the United Kingdom. He or she appoints a cabinet of up to twenty-one ministers and together they conduct the business of the nation. The cabinet includes the chancellor of the exchequer—the minister who presents the annual budget on the country's finances—and ministers representing the government departments in charge of home affairs, foreign affairs, education, and health, among others.

The prime minister is typically the leader of the political party that holds the largest number of seats in the House of Commons. Those seats are held by elected officials, and elections must be held no more than five years apart. In 2010, David Cameron, leader of the Conservative Party, became prime minister through 2015, when elections would next be held.

PARLIAMENT The United Kingdom has a bicameral, or two-house, parliamentary system made up of the House of Lords and the House of Commons.

The House of Commons, or lower house, has 650 elected Members of Parliament (MPs) representing constituencies—533 in England, forty in Wales, fifty-nine in Scotland, and eighteen in Northern Ireland. Each constituency has approximately 50,000 to 80,000 voters. The members debate and pass bills before sending the legislation to the House of Lords.

Proceedings in the House of Commons are chaired by the Speaker, who recognizes MPs in turn and keeps order in the sometimes unruly debates. The prime minister has to face Parliament each week to face questions on the running of the country. Parliamentary debates are televised, reported on the radio, and recorded verbatim. Parliamentary committees are formed to investigate policies, with members of different political parties taking part. The Public Accounts Committee, for example, questions the government's spending policies.

The House of Lords, or the upper house, debates those bills that have passed the House of Commons, and its role is generally to give assent to their passage. Debate is more leisurely and gentlemanly than in the House of Commons. The number of members, or peers, is not fixed; in October 2014 the House of Lords had 789. The House of Lords has not historically been a representative body and consists of the Lords Spiritual (the two archbishops and other bishops of the Anglican Church), the Law Lords (those at the head of the legal system), and the Lords Temporal (those appointed based on outstanding deeds, especially in public life, and with a noble or aristocratic background). Once bills have passed through both the House of Commons and the House of Lords, the monarch gives Royal Assent to them before they become law.

REGIONAL GOVERNMENT

In 1999 a significant amount of governing power was transferred from the central government in Westminster to the different regions of the United Kingdom. Called devolution, this decentralization of government was implemented by Prime Minister Tony Blair's Labour government to placate increasing nationalist sentiments, especially in Scotland, and to enable each region to deal with specific needs and circumstances. However, the UK government retains control over foreign policy, defense, and economic and monetary systems, among others.

Scotland's First Minister Nicola Sturgeon announces her plan for government to the Scottish Parliament in 2014 in Edinburgh.

Scotland now has its own parliament of 129 members, called members of the Scottish Parliament (MSPs), in Edinburgh. It can pass laws on education, health, agriculture, transportation, and justice matters, as well as on income tax. Its policies include free long-term personal care for the elderly and no tuition fees for students in higher education.

Wales has its own National Assembly in Cardiff with sixty elected members. Prior to 2006, the Welsh assembly did not have the law-making or taxing powers that the Scottish Parliament had. The Government of Wales Act 2006 sought to remedy that, conferring to the Assembly certain legislative powers. Further empowerment was granted following a referendum in 2011, and the process appears to be ongoing. Some initiatives that differ from Westminster include free bus travel for senior citizens, extended support for the homeless, and free medical prescriptions for those under twenty-five years of age.

POLITICAL PARTIES

United Kingdom Independence Party leader, Nigel Farage (R), leads demonstrators outside the House of Commons in London in a 2014 lobby against EU arrest warrant policies.

While there have always been several political parties represented in Parliament, since World War II the government of Britain has been split between the Conservative Party and the Labour Party. The Conservative Party is committed to encouraging business through lower direct taxes, controlling inflation by limiting government spending, and bringing private enterprise to state-run utilities and infrastructure. By contrast, the Labour Party has historically held more socialist values, championing workers' rights, investing to generate employment, and investing heavily in public services.

The Liberal Democratic Party, the third main political party, occupies the central political ground between the Conservative and Labour parties. The Green Party, formerly the Ecology Party, enjoys small but growing support for its environmental policies.

REGIONAL POLITICS

WALES *Plaid Cymru* (PLY-d KUM-ee), the Welsh nationalist party, was founded in 1925 and became active in the 1970s. It has helped Wales to gain its own television and radio channels, to reintroduce the Welsh language into schools in the 1970s, to post bilingual Welsh and English road signs and government publications, and to demand devolution and the creation of the Welsh Assembly in Cardiff.

SCOTLAND The Scottish National Party also championed Scottish devolution from England and was the official opposition in the first Scottish parliament in Edinburgh. The Scottish National Party and Plaid Cymru want their countries to become independent national members of the European Union.

THE LEGAL SYSTEM

Britain has an uncodified constitution—there is no single document. It relies on a large body of precedent cases, or "common law," that has been built up since the eleventh century. In addition, there is legislation passed by Parliament, known as equity law, and law passed by the European Community, which in many cases takes precedence over British domestic law. There are three divisions to the legal system in the United Kingdom: that of England and Wales, that of Scotland, and that of Northern Ireland.

In England and Wales, less serious criminal cases are tried first in magistrates' or local courts. Some large cities also have paid full-time stipendiary magistrates, who sit alone and decide cases. More serious cases are referred to the crown courts. There are ninety-three of these in England and Wales, each presided over by a judge with a jury of twelve citizens to assess guilt and pass sentences. The Central Criminal Court in London is the ultimate criminal court, while the Royal Courts of Justice is the ultimate civil court. Legal aid, paid for by public funds, is available for victims of crimes and for criminal defendants but is not available for civil cases. The Home Secretary has overall responsibility for the criminal justice system. Northern Ireland's court system is similar to that of England and Wales.

In Scotland, most minor criminal cases are tried informally in police courts in the towns and in magistrates' courts in the countryside. More serious criminal cases are tried in the sheriff courts, where the sheriff sits alone for minor cases and with a jury for more serious cases.

A British police officer stands watch outside the House of Parliament in London.

SCOTLAND CONSIDERS INDEPENDENCE

Should Scotland be an independent country? More than four million Scots answered that question when they voted in the 2014 Scottish Independence Referendum. The Kingdom of Scotland was an independent country many centuries ago, but has been joined with Great Britain in one way or another, on and off, since 1603, and without a break since 1707.

Nevertheless, in the twentieth century, many Scots wondered if the time had come again for Scotland to be its own nation, politically free of any bonds to England and its United Kingdom. After all, Ireland had left the United Kingdom in 1922 and by 1948 had established itself fully as the independent country it is today. (Ireland's northern counties, called Northern Ireland, remain part of the UK) If Ireland could go it alone, why not Scotland?

In 2007, the Scottish National Party, headed by Scottish First Minister Alex Salmond, opened a "National Conversation" on the topic of independence that eventually led to the referendum on September 18, 2014. The British government announced it would abide by whatever the Scottish people decided, but hoped that Scotland would remain as part of the United Kingdom. People on both sides of the issue formed campaign groups—"Yes Scotland" (supporters pictured here) was for independence, and "Better Together" was opposed. As in any important democratic election, this one spawned billboards, television commercials, and heated debates in the months leading up to the vote.

Although the question asked of voters was a simple one, requiring only a "yes" or "no" answer, it was a deeply emotional and complex issue. A win for the affirmative would create many complicated problems in the disentangling of Scotland from the rest of the United Kingdom—especially in terms of defense and the economy. Such a move would require profound changes

in how an independent Scotland would provide for its citizens and how it would interact with the rest of the world. Nevertheless, voters who favored independence did so out of a sense of patriotism and the conviction that only the Scots themselves should determine their country's policies and future. Those who opposed independence believed they were better off as part of a larger, stronger political entity.

In the end, Scotland voted to remain a part of the United Kingdom. Out of an electorate of 4,283,392 Scottish voters, 44.7 percent voted yes and 55.3 percent voted no, with an impressive 84.6 percent turning out to have their say.

Whether there will ever be another such vote remains to be seen, but most observers agree that it's unlikely anytime soon. However, in accordance with the Scotland Act 2012, from which the referendum resulted, certain powers were to be passed, or devolved, from the British government to the Scottish Parliament. In other words, Scotland came out of this process with more political power in the UK.

INTERNET LINKS

www.gov.uk/government/topical-events/scottish-independence-referendum

This page on the official UK government website explains the Scottish independence referendum and its results.

www.parliament.uk

The official website of the UK Parliament has government news and information as well as an excellent "Education" section.

www.scottish.parliament.uk

The site of the Scottish Parliament explains how the government works, but has much more as well.

wales.gov.uk

The site of the Welsh government covers a wide range of topics.

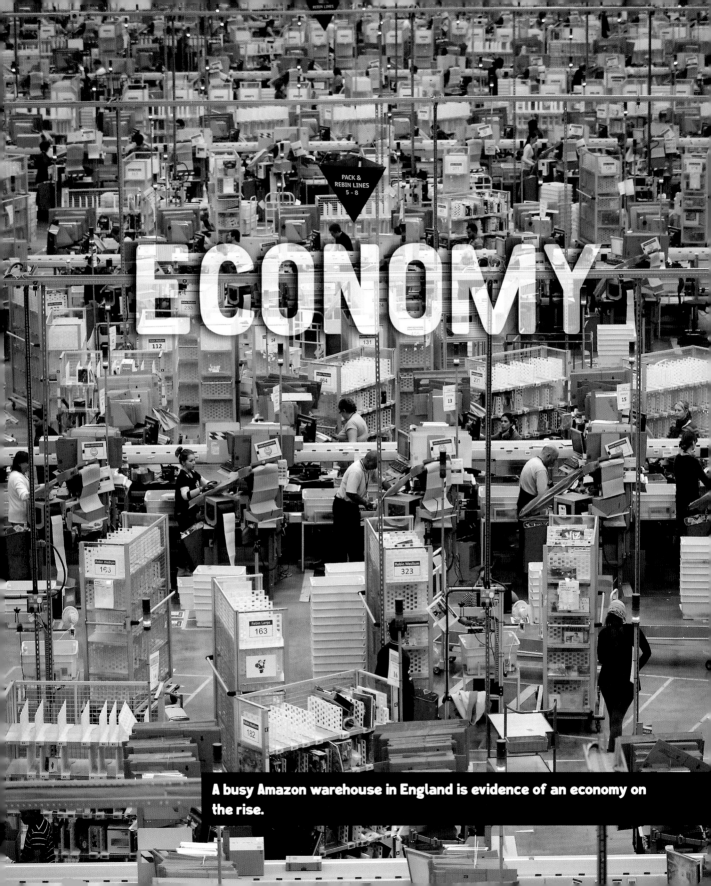

ECONOMY

A busy Amazon warehouse in England is evidence of an economy on the rise.

4

THE ECONOMY OF GREAT BRITAIN is usually discussed in terms of the entire United Kingdom. Although each of the four countries has its own economic situation, the UK is considered one economy—the sixth-largest national economy in the world and the third-largest in Europe, as measured by gross domestic product (GDP). GDP is a statistic that economists use to measure a country's economic well-being. Typically, the higher a country's GDP number, the better off that nation and its people tend to be.

This Aston Martin is displayed as part of the company's 100th anniversary celebration in 2013 in Gaydon, England.

With its mountainous landscape and many sandy beaches, Wales attracts a large number of tourists. Cardiff is the most popular destination for visitors to Wales, with 14.6 million visitors in 2009. Scotland is also a popular tourist destination, not only for its scenic beauty and historic sites, but also for golf—the country has 550 golf courses!

As the economy recovers, shoppers return to the stores, like these women in London.

As a member of the EU, the UK benefits from a large market for manufactured and agricultural goods. Together with the United States, Japan, Canada, Germany, France, Italy, and Russia, the UK is one of the world's eight leading industrial nations (G8).

The UK entered the twenty-first century in strong economic condition, following a long period of sustained economic growth, low inflation, low interest rates, and high employment. Then the global economic crisis hit in 2008, and the economy went into a nosedive, or to be more precise, a recession. A recession is defined as "a period of reduced economic activity," which sounds mild, but in reality the 2008–2009 recession caused tremendous hardship for many people. During that time, the UK economy shrank by 7.2 percent. Investors lost money and many people lost jobs. In one year, unemployment rose from 5.2 percent in 2008 to 7.6 percent in 2009.

Since then, British leaders have instituted measures to improve the situation, but recovery has been slow. In 2013, the unemployment rate was 7.2 percent, but the economy grew by 1.99 percent, its strongest rate since 2007, and growth continued through 2014.

MANUFACTURING

HEAVY INDUSTRY Britain's heavy manufacturing industry originally developed close to sources of power. For example, heavy engineering, steel production, manufacturing for the oil industry, shipbuilding, and ship repair facilities developed near the Northumberland and Durham coalfields. In nearby Teeside, a chemical industry developed to turn coal by-products, chemicals from the Tees salt field, and oil refinery by-products into paints, fertilizers, explosives, plastics, and textiles. Steel production boomed in South Wales and Sheffield, areas with adjacent coalfields.

However, the UK's industry sector has been shrinking as the services sector grows. In 1948, British industry (including manufacturing, oil and gas extraction, and utilities) accounted for 41 percent of the British economy. By 2013, it was just 14 percent. About 2.6 million people are directly employed in manufacturing, with many more in related supply chains, services, and transportation industries.

Aston Martin employees check nearly finished cars in the factory.

AUTOMOTIVE INDUSTRY Automobiles are a large source of manufactured exports. The UK is best known for premium and sports car brands including Aston Martin, Bentley, Daimler, Jaguar, Lagonda, Land Rover, Lotus, McLaren, MG, Mini, Morgan—and Rolls-Royce, which is also the world's second-largest aircraft engine maker.

OTHER SECTORS Britain's aerospace sector is one of the world's largest, employing around 113,000 people and many more indirectly. The construction sector employed about 2.2 million in 2009, and supported 194,000 construction firms. The island's largest construction project is Crossrail, a 73-mile (118-km) railway, with 26 miles (42 km) of new tunnels, running east to west through London and into the surrounding countryside, with a branch to Heathrow Airport. It is due to open in 2018.

Pharmaceuticals are another large industry, with the British companies GlaxoSmithKline and AstraZeneca at the helm. Creative industries, such as the arts, design, publishing, advertising, software, toys and games, are other important sectors. Britain's fashion industry, for example, contributed £26 billion ($40.85 billion) to the UK economy in 2014.

Britain was the world's first industrialized country, the place where the Industrial Revolution first began. As the population grew, its demand for clothes, goods, and houses increased as well. New scientific discoveries and inventions led to a radical change in manufacturing methods that is now called the Industrial Revolution. Instead of doing handwork at home, workers at machines in factories produced large numbers of goods, and Britain became "the workshop of the world."

The revolution started in the textile industry. James Hargreaves' spinning jenny of the 1760s spun thread on multiple spinning wheels; Richard Arkwright's water frame further refined spinning and harnessed water power successfully while Samuel Crompton's mule-jenny combined the two. Edmund Cartwright invented a power loom in 1785 that used animal power at first and steam power later.

Abraham Darby's invention of the coke-smelting process in Coalbrookdale in 1709 enabled Britain to use its large natural deposits of iron, while Henry Cort invented a "puddling" process for making wrought or malleable iron, as opposed to cast iron. He also invented a rolling mill. Darby's grandson built the first iron bridge across the Severn at

"Coalbookdale by Night" by Philip James de Loutherbourg, 1801, shows industrial activity.

Ironbridge, which opened in 1779. In the 1780s, the first iron ship was built, as were cast-iron pipes for city water systems.

The coal industry also benefited from scientific inventions. In the early 1700s, a steam pump helped to drain pits. This was refined by James Watt into the steam engine in 1769. Steam power was used for draining and hauling in the coal industry, and further improvements in propping, lighting, and ventilation developed during the nineteenth century. The steam engine was adopted by other manufacturing industries and formed the basis of Stephenson's Rocket, *the first steam locomotive, in 1829 that triggered the mid-nineteenth-century railway boom. Engineering and machine tool industries also developed.*

The growth of new industrial towns such as Manchester, with their own merchant classes, led to major social change and growing political demands. Working conditions in factories and coal pits were dangerous and highly exploitative but gradually improved during the nineteenth and twentieth centuries.

THE SERVICES SECTOR

In 2014, 77.8 percent of Britain's labor force worked in the services sector. This category includes education, health, and social services; financial and business services; tourism, hotels, and restaurants; transport, storage, and communications; and the wholesale and retail trades.

The National Health Service, the main provider of health care in Britain, is publicly funded, and is the largest employer in Europe, with a workforce of around 1.7 million. The NHS operates independently in each of the four countries of the UK, with the NHS in England being the largest of the four parts. Its budget in 2013/14 was £110 billion ($173.7 billion).

Medical systems and pharmaceuticals are other important businesses in this sector. Britain supplies a quarter of the world market's single-use disposable products. In addition, business services, insurance, marketing and advertising, market research, conference and exhibition organization, and management consultancy are all growth areas.

FINANCE AND BANKING

Great Britain is a leading international financial services center, employing two million people and hosting some five hundred foreign banks. The London Stock Exchange is a major trading center—Eurobonds, stocks, and funds are traded in London and Manchester. The Bank of England is the government's banker and prints bank notes.

The London Stock Exchange is an important player in global economy.

CURRENCY Although the UK is a part of the European Union, it is not a member of the Eurozone, the economic and monetary union of the EU. That's because the UK chose not to adopt the euro as its national currency, and instead continues to use the pound sterling, its traditional currency. The euro was introduced as a new single currency system for Europe in 2002, replacing the individual currencies used by most European countries, such as the French franc.

AGRICULTURE

Seventy-one percent of Britain's land area is used for agriculture, with 12 percent woodlands. British agriculture provides about 60 percent of the public's food needs, but contributes a mere 0.7 percent to the UK's GDP, and is therefore not a major economic sector. About two thirds of production is devoted to livestock, and one-third to crops. Only 1.4 percent of the workforce is employed in farming.

Wheat is the most widely grown crop; other important crops include barley, with its by-product malt that is used in the production of beer and whiskey, and oilseed rape, used for making vegetable oil. Other crops include sugar beets and potatoes.

Britain has 2.3 million dairy cows, which produce about 4 billion gallons (14 billion liters) of milk per year. Half of this milk is processed into cheese and other products. Pigs and sheep are widely farmed; the United Kingdom is the one of the largest wool producers in the world.

Since the 1990s there has been a growing trend toward organic farming, which uses less intensive methods and no artificial fertilizers or pesticides.

Sheep graze on a farm in the Peak District.

INTERNET LINKS

www.economywatch.com/world_economy/united-kingdom
Economy Watch, "The Economy of the UK, GB, British Isles (or Whatever You Want to Call It!)," is a relatively easy-to-understand overview of the UK economy with a large graphic for easy illustration.

www.theguardian.com/business/economics-blog/2014/apr/24/uk-economy-seven-things-need-to-know-ons-g7
The Guardian article, "Seven things you need to know about the UK economy," is a short and direct overview of the subject.

www.ukagriculture.com
UKAgriculture is the top agriculture, food, and farming resource.

ENVIRONMENT

London is notorious for its traffic, which adds to the city's air pollution problem.

5

BEING A MEMBER OF THE EUROPEAN Union, the United Kingdom is expected to meet the environmental standards that the EU sets for all its member states. Britain's environmental concerns are similar to those faced by most industrialized countries, and the government is actively involved in cleaning up problem areas and promoting a healthier, cleaner land. The main agencies responsible for environmental protection in Great Britain are the Department for the Environment, Food, and Rural Affairs (DEFRA), the Environment Agency, and the Scottish Environmental Protection Agency, which all work closely together.

AIR POLLUTION

Air pollution causes cancer and leads to some twenty-nine thousand premature deaths in the UK each year. It is the number one environmental killer not only in Britain but throughout the EU. Air quality in Wales and

Great Britain was once covered in woodland, but farming and the need for timber almost wiped out the island's forests. Today about 12 percent of Britain's land is wooded, and the area is increasing. In 1919, only 5 percent of the land was wooded, and a century later the recovery is still in progress. Other European countries average from 25 to 37 percent of their area as woodland.

To reduce both traffic and air pollution, children often travel to school via walking bus, in which they wear reflective vests and stay behind their "driver."

Scotland, while not perfect, tends to be better than in England.

Motor vehicles are the greatest source of nitrogen dioxide (NO_2) emissions in Britain. In 2014, the European Commission, the executive body of the European Union, launched legal proceedings against the UK for failing to reduce excessive levels of NO_2 air pollution from traffic. This sort of air pollution causes major respiratory problems and is a particular problem in the Greater London area, as well as in other sections of England. London has the highest levels of NO_2 of any European capital city. In 1999, London set a target clean air standard, but now says it won't be able to reach that standard until 2025 at the earliest.

Other sources of pollution include power stations, which produce 70 percent of Britain's sulphur dioxide emissions—responsible for acid rain—and large landfills, which contribute methane. In 2008, the UK was the world's ninth greatest producer of human-made carbon emissions, generated from fossil fuels; it produced around 1.8 percent of the total worldwide. Carbon emissions contribute to global warming.

WATER POLLUTION

As with air quality, the EU issues directives on member states' water quality. Britain has made great progress in cleaning up its inland and coastal waterways to meet those standards. Rivers and lakes, groundwater, and beaches can be polluted by agricultural and urban sources, discharges of sewage effluent, storm water overflows, and river-borne microorganisms—all of which can have a significant impact on human health.

THE LONDON CONGESTION CHARGE

In February 2003 the mayor of London, Ken Livingstone, introduced a congestion charge of £5 ($9) a day on all vehicles entering an area of central London between 7 a.m. and 6:30 p.m. on weekdays. The intention of the Congestion Zone was to reduce the number of motor vehicles in the area and relieve traffic congestion. A secondary effect, officials hoped, would be a reduction in air pollution.

By 2014, the congestion charge had risen to £11.50 ($18) a day. It has been difficult to assess the law's results, because it's impossible to tease apart the different direct causes and their effects. In 2013, a ten-year study of the impact of the Congestion Charge concluded that, in general, the policy had resulted in fewer cars, less pollution, and a positive impact on health.

The island's drinking water is of the highest quality, with England, Wales, and Scotland all reporting close to 100 percent compliance with the strict UK and EU standards in 2013—2014. While the region's beaches are in generally good condition, the UK government reports that only 27 percent of England's water bodies are classified as being of "good status" and is working to meet the objectives of the EU's Water Framework Directive.

ENERGY AND THE ENVIRONMENT

Britain's energy is derived predominantly from fossil fuels. Coal, oil, and natural gas are all used in power stations to produce electricity. Rigorous

London is transforming its traditional telephone booths into solar-powered charging stations.

emissions standards and regulations are enforced, in compliance with national and EU laws and international guidelines.

Britain's nuclear power industry supplies around 20 percent of the country's electricity, but its existing nuclear power plants are reaching the ends of their productive lives. In October 2014, EU authorities approved a plan for a new nuclear power station in southwest England, Britain's first new plant since the mid-1990s. To meet climate change goals, the UK government is encouraging the construction of nuclear power stations as well as renewable energy installations such as giant offshore wind farms and projects using tidal power. Renewable energy provided 11.3 percent of Britain's energy output in 2012.

CLIMATE CHANGE

Britain is a major supporter of the Kyoto Protocol, an agreement among industrialized nations to reduce greenhouse-gas emissions, and is implementing measures to reduce further damage to the ozone layer and thus slow down global warming. The country is also a key member of the Intergovernmental Panel on Climate Change, a scientific organization under the auspices of the United Nations.

Weather scientists predict that global warming will cause an increase of extreme weather events in Great Britain. They also expect the island to have wetter, milder winters, on average, and hotter, drier summers.

Already, Britain has recently seen highly variable weather, with a drought in early 2012 and the wettest winter for England and Wales in 250 years between 2013 and 2014, which led to widespread flooding. Up to 10 percent of Britain's total land area, inhabited by six million people, is a flood plain, and flooding has become more frequent. At the current rate of climate change, London's flood defenses will need to be redesigned or replaced by 2030. In addition, coastal erosion threatens significant parts of the eastern coasts.

WILDLIFE CONSERVATION

A system of national parks, conservation areas, places of outstanding natural beauty, and green belts near cities ensure a balance between the immediate needs of Britain's people and the protection of wildlife and natural habitats. Changing agricultural practices have reduced the number of hedgerows in some areas, while nitrate fertilizers increase crop yield at the expense of birds and small mammals. Lowland heaths, traditional grasslands, and salt marshes are all declining.

There is a mixed picture of decline and recovery for Britain's wildlife. Among the top ten endangered animals in the British Isles are the Scottish wildcat—Britain's last large mammal predator—the cuckoo, the turtledove and the beloved and very British red squirrel and hedgehog.

Between 10 and 20 percent of indigenous species of freshwater fish, nonmarine reptiles and amphibians, and seed plants are endangered. Approximately 220 different species of birds nest in Britain, of which 139 species are in decline.

In parts of Great Britain, hedgehogs are in such great danger from motor vehicles that special tunnels are created to help them cross the road safely.

European Robin

England's beloved red robin, also called robin redbreast, is a small gray-brown bird with a bright orange breast. Though it is often called an English robin, it's actually a European robin, or Erithacus rubecula. *Orinthologists, or bird experts, classify this robin as a member of the bird family called Old World flycatcher.*

Interestingly, the bird acquired the name "redbreast" despite its orange coloring because the word orange *did not come into use until the sixteenth century. That's when the fruit was first introduced to Europe from Asia. The color was named after the fruit and the first known recorded use of the English word* orange *as a color dates to 1512. By that time, however, the name of the redbreast bird was long established. The redbreast picked up the additional name robin in the fifteenth century; Robin was already a human name at the time.*

The American robin is a completely different bird. The Turdus migratorius *is a migratory songbird of the thrush family. It is one of the most common of North American birds.*

When British people settled in America, they found that the English robin did not exist on the continent. However, a slightly larger thrush with a reddish breast was common, and they called it a robin instead. The term robin *for the American species has been recorded since at least 1703. The American robin is not found outside of North America, and is therefore not seen in England.*

American Robin

Over 70 percent of Britain's fish stocks are either fully or over-exploited. A 2010 study found that in England and Wales, the amount of fish being caught in the nineteenth century was four times greater than current levels. Since 1889, stocks of halibut, turbot, haddock, and plaice have been depleted by 94 percent; cod has fallen by 87 per cent. Fish stocks are regulated by internationally agreed fishing quotas, and bad fishing practices such as the use of drift nets, which catch dolphins and other sea mammals unintentionally, have been stopped. Britain is a leading member of the International Whaling Commission and is strongly opposed to any kind of whaling.

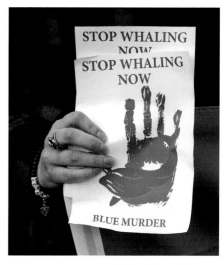

While the anti-whaling laws in Great Britain are secure, this protestor outside of the Norwegian embassy in London, is trying to ensure the whales' safety elsewhere.

INTERNET LINKS

www.forestry.gov.uk
The Forestry Commissions of England, Scotland, and Wales have helpful websites.

www.gov.uk/government/organisations/environment-agency
This government site covers a broad range of environmental topics.

www.doncaster.gov.uk/airq/focus_on/acid_rain.asp
Fresh Air addresses a variety of air pollution topics relevant to Great Britain.

www.gov.uk/government/policies/improving-water-quality
This government page explains how the UK is addressing water pollution issues.

www.sepa.org.uk
The Scottish Environmental Protection Agency works to protect and improve Scotland's air, land, and water.

THE BRITISH

Camilla, the Duchess of Cornwall, and her husband Prince Charles, the Prince of Wales, wave to the public on a visit to Cornwall.

6

I N THE UNITED KINGDOM'S 2011 census, a population survey taken every ten years, there was no listing for people to check for Cornish as their national identity. (Cornwall is a peninsula in the southwesternmost part of England, the traditional homeland of the Cornish people, and one of the "Celtic nations"—a territory where a distinct Celtic cultural identity remains.) This was despite the fact that thousands of the people living in Cornwall had manually written "Cornish" on the 2001 census form, rather than check the boxes for "British" or "English."

In advance of the new census, Cornish activists worked to inform residents that they could identify themselves as Cornish by writing it in the national identity, ethnicity, and main language sections. Additionally, people could record "Cornwall" as their country of birth. In 2014, the UK government announced that it would recognize Cornish as a national minority.

This story illustrates how people in Britain generally consider themselves Welsh, Scottish, Irish, English, West Indian, or Bangladeshi rather than British. Local or regional loyalties often supersede national

Just as there is a census of the British people, England holds an annual census of its swans. By tradition, the Queen owns all of the mute swans on the River Thames. Each year, the swans are counted in a "swan upping," an event which dates to the twelfth century. They are then examined and banded by the royal swan warden.

ones. The population is diverse, especially in the urban areas of Greater London and the West Midlands. Some 8 million people in Britain, or roughly 13 percent of the country's population, belong to a minority ethnic group.

THE EARLIEST SETTLERS

Britain, like the United States, has a long and proud history of immigration. Some of the people living in Cornwall, Wales, and western Scotland can trace their ancestry back to the Celtic tribes that populated these areas more than ten centuries ago.

Angles, Saxons, and Vikings all left their mark in a Celto-Roman gene pool, augmented by the invading Normans in 1066. Migrations throughout the European continent over the centuries also added to the British mixture. The migrants included weavers from Flanders, Huguenots (Protestants) who were expelled from France by Louis XIV, refugees fleeing from continental wars during the sixteenth and seventeenth centuries, and French nobles fleeing the extremes of the French Revolution in the eighteenth century.

A tiny citizen runs up a hill in the English countryside.

IMMIGRANTS

In the 2011 census, 7.5 million people, or 11.9 percent of the total population, reported being foreign born. The largest number came from India, a former British colony, followed by Poland, making Poles the third-largest foreign-born community after the Irish and Indian.

Britain's Jewish community dates to the eleventh century. Many major merchant banks and stockbrokerage houses were founded by Jewish families. Jews came from Central Europe, Hungary, Poland, and Russia in the nineteenth century, and from Nazi Germany in the twentieth century.

After World War II, Britain enticed laborers from its colonies to help in the postwar reconstruction at home. The S.S. *Empire Windrush* carried the first skilled and semiskilled West Indian workers in 1948. Immigration from the

Caribbean colonies increased from 11,000 in 1954 to 34,000 in 1962, after the United States introduced immigration controls in the early 1950s.

The majority of Britain's West Indian population settled in Greater London. Thousands of South Asian immigrants from India, Pakistan, and Bangladesh arrived in the 1950s, settling in Greater London and in manufacturing towns with acute labor shortages. Ugandan president Idi Amin's expulsion of Asians in 1972 drove 27,000 highly trained and talented people of Pakistani descent to Britain.

Approximately 430,000 Chinese, mainly from Hong Kong, have also set up small businesses and entered professions in Britain. London has a Chinatown, and most towns throughout England now have Chinese takeout restaurants. Vietnamese people fleeing their Communist government were initially accepted in the early 1980s, but immigration controls have since tightened. Immigration increased in the 1990s from Eastern Europe and the Balkans, especially during the conflicts in Bosnia and Kosovo. Wherever there is conflict in the world, many of those who are able to leave choose to go to Britain.

A police officer walks past a flag-draped barrier at the Port of Dover in Dover, England, in 2014. Demonstrators there called for greater security to protect truck drivers from migrants trying to enter Britain illegally from France.

RACIAL DISCRIMINATION AND INTEGRATION

Demonstrators in Trafalgar Square in London rally against incitement and Islamophobia.

There are strict laws regarding employment and civil equality in Britain. It is illegal to advertise job vacancies on the basis of color, creed, or sex, and the Commission for Racial Equality can take employers to court for discriminatory practices. The Race Relations (Amendment) Act of 2000 requires that major public organizations promote racial equality. In 2010, twenty-seven out of 650 members of Parliament came from ethnic minorities.

Intolerance of immigrants and support for extremist right-wing organizations has been strongest in the poorer inner-city areas. Immigration and customs officials and police officers seem to detain a disproportionate number of people of color for questioning, and a few notorious civil cases have shown alarming prejudice among some police forces. Tensions and unrest have occasionally boiled over.

Perhaps the most noticeable challenge to civil equality in Britain today is not one of race or ethnicity but of religion and culture. So-called "Islamophobia," or fear of Muslims, is a social phenomenon that has grown

MALE PRIMOGENITURE

The rule of male primogeniture is an ancient custom that values men over women. This rule governs the inheritance of class position and family estates among the British aristocracy. Of the approximately one thousand aristocratic titles in Great Britain, only about ninety can be passed on to daughters. All others can be passed only to sons.

If a nobleman has sons, the inheritance goes to the firstborn. If the man has daughters, but no son, he cannot pass his title and estate on to a daughter. He must find a male relative, even a distant one, to whom he can pass the title or it will essentially be put on hold, or even terminated.

Male primogeniture conflicts with modern thinking, so some wonder why it remains in an otherwise progressive nation. In fact, the royal succession to the throne was always passed according to the principle of male primogeniture, but in 2013, the rule was altered to allow a firstborn female to succeed to the throne. The old system remains, however, for the aristocracy. After all, if the concept of equality were to be applied to the inheritance of class privilege, it could highlight the unfairness of the entire system. Aristocracy in itself is a concept based on the inequality between the classes. Therefore, some aristocrats believe it's better to leave well enough alone.

The boys of Eton College take part in the morning assembly. The prestigious school was founded in 1440 by King Henry VI.

out of tensions between the West and Islamic nations in recent years. In Britain, violence and terror attacks by Muslim extremists have exacerbated the problem, while law-abiding Muslims bear the brunt of discrimination and harassment.

CLASS DIVISIONS

Distinctions of accent, word usage, topics of conversation, upbringing, table manners, dress, general deportment, meal times, and preferences for food, drink, and entertainment—all these are clues by which one British person might size up another's class and place in society.

At the top of the ladder, second only to the monarchy, is the aristocracy. Members have dwindling economic power but enjoy tremendous vestigial influence and respect. The titled aristocracy is made up of dukes, marquises, earls, viscounts, and barons. All pass their positions, called peerage, to their children when they die, but for the most part, the peerage is passed almost exclusively to male offspring.

A paternalistic outlook, a sense of guardianship of property, and a duty to perform public service are widespread attributes of this class. Twice a year, life peers are created by the monarch from all walks of life, in recognition of their contribution to their field or profession. This privilege enables the holder to a seat in the House of Lords, but those titles cannot be passed on to the next generation.

Among the middle classes, there are numerous subtle gradations. The upper middle classes may earn money in the professions, but many members of this class have inherited wealth as well. The higher echelons of political and economic power and all walks of public life are still dominated by those who attended one of Britain's exclusive schools—Eton in particular—and either Oxford or Cambridge University. Parents of all social classes would like to be able to provide such educational advantages for their own children.

However, old divisions and categories are being eroded, and new ones are taking their place. Inheritance taxes, high labor costs, and falling markets for agricultural products have hit members of the aristocracy hard. Sports stars, celebrities, and other high-profile personalities, whose wealth and fame far outreach that of most aristocrats, are increasingly seen as the top tier of society. At the other end of the spectrum, government initiatives have helped to reduce poverty, but the social divisions between the richest and the poorest remain enormous.

INTERNET LINKS

www.theguardian.com/uk-news/2014/apr/26/survival-of-cornish-identity-cornwall-separate-place
"Cornish identity: why Cornwall has always been a separate place" is a fascinating 2014 article from *The Guardian*.

www.debretts.com/people/essential-guide-peerage
Debrett's is an excellent source for information about British society and social etiquette. The sections on peerage and titles explain aristocratic hierarchies.

www.ons.gov.uk/ons/guide-method/census/2011/index.html
The Office for National Statistics Census 2011 is a section on Britain's most recent census.

LIFESTYLE

A piper leades a bride and groom in a traditional wedding procession in Applecross in the Highlands of Scotland.

7

A CCORDING TO THE 2014 PROSPERITY Index, issued annually by the London-based Legatum Institute, Great Britain was the thirteenth happiest place on Earth. Naturally, happiness can't be quantified like that, but by comparing statistics about a country's wealth and well-being, it's possible to come up with a ranking of prosperity, which is equated with a population's overall happiness. While number thirteen is certainly not number one (that honor belonged to Norway), it's not bad, out of a pool of 142. In fact, Britain placed higher than most of its European neighbors. In general, the British lifestyle is good.

In 2014, the name Muhammad (with its various spellings) topped the charts as the most popular boys' name for newborn British babies, surpassing the previous favorites Oliver and Jack. This is an indication of the impact of a growing Muslim population on British society. Among girls' names, the Arabic name Nur was number twenty-nine, in its first showing on the Top 100 list.

MARRIAGE AND FAMILY LIFE

In England and Wales, marriage is legal at age sixteen, but requires parental permission for people under eighteen. In Scotland, the minimum age is also sixteen, but requires no parental permission. Same-sex marriage is legal in England, Scotland, and Wales following legislation passed in 2013 and 2014.

Most children live in two-parent families, but the number of single-parent families is growing. In 2011, 26 percent of families with children were headed by a single parent, of which 92 percent were women. One of the factors affecting that situation is the divorce rate, which is one of the highest in Europe, with 2.8 divorces for every one thousand people.

Protesters gather outside the Houses of Parliament in central London on June 3, 2013, in support of same-sex marriage.

Teen pregnancy is also a factor, and a concern, with Britain having the highest teen pregnancy rate in Europe. The good news, however, is that the teen pregnancy rate has fallen almost 10 percent since 1969. In 2012, about three of every one hundred girls ages fifteen to seventeen became pregnant in England, Wales, and Scotland. Public health officials point to the success of concerted efforts over the past decade or so to bring the teen pregnancy rate down, with educational and health programs both in and out of school, but say more work needs to be done.

CHILDHOOD

In general, the British have small nuclear families. Similar to other industrialized countries, the birth rate in Britain is declining. Many aspects of British life are similar to those in other Western countries.

Most babies are born in hospitals or birth centers run by midwives. Childcare remains predominantly the mother's concern, but there are also many men who stay home to take care of the children while their wives work.

THE ROYAL FAMILY

Perhaps nothing exemplifies Great Britain more than the British royal family. Although the king or queen's role is now mostly ceremonial, the royalty is still considered tremendously important. Members of the royal family perform many public duties, such as heading charities, meeting with dignitaries, greeting the public, giving speeches, and attending state ceremonies.

Elizabeth II became queen in 1952 at the age of twenty-five. On Sept. 9, 2015, the queen will surpass the record set by her great-great-grandmother Queen Victoria, who reigned from 1837 to 1901, as the longest-reigning monarch in British history (sixty-three years, seven months). Some say Elizabeth II has been the most popular and most dutiful monarch in a thousand years. However, as the queen becomes increasingly aged, it is clear the crown must soon pass to her son, Prince Charles.

Although some in Britain advocate for an end to the monarchy—a movement called Republicanism—recent polls show that 75 to 80 percent of the public favor keeping it. In fact, most British genuinely love their royals and many people eagerly follow the latest royal news. A royal wedding—such as the 2011 wedding of the queen's grandson Prince William and Catherine Middleton—is a huge affair. The birth of their son Prince George in 2013 and subsequent news of an expected second child in 2015 received a joyous popular response.

Prince George on his first birthday.

ON... IN TH...

STOP POVERTY

Students rally in Parliament Square to highlight the plight of the UK's poorest children as supporters on a Save the Children bus passes behind them.

Economic pressures are especially heavy burdens to low-income and even middle-income families with young children. Preschool childcare is expensive, and parents who cannot afford it are less likely to be able to work. The government subsidizes early childhood education and childcare in various ways, but policymakers are looking for ways to simplify, extend, and provide more equity in its childcare support programs.

Poverty is the most serious problem facing British children. One recent study concluded that there are almost 300,000 households in Great Britain where none of the adults has ever worked. And about 300,000 children have parents with serious drug problems. Children in families affected by problems of poverty, drug abuse, violence, and mental illness—problems that frequently overlap—have reduced chances of success in their own lives.

Health officials are also concerned about the increasing problem of childhood obesity in Great Britain, calling the situation a "state of emergency." The National Child Measurement Programme measures the height and weight of around one million school children in England every year. Between

2012 and 2013, more than one-quarter of those children aged two to fifteen were found to be either obese or overweight, with slightly higher numbers for Scottish children, and the figures for Welsh children being the highest at about one-third.

Queen Elizabeth II visits students at St Mary and St Pancras Church of England Primary School in London.

EDUCATION

Education is free and compulsory for all children between the ages of five and eighteen. Schools are divided into primary (ages five—eleven) and secondary (ages eleven—eighteen) schools, with a national curriculum having achievement tests at various grade levels. The major exams are the General Certificate of Secondary Education (GCSE) taken at age sixteen, (in Scotland, it's the Scottish Certificate of Education) and the Advanced (A) Level exam at age seventeen or eighteen. Some schools now offer the International Baccalaureate qualification instead of A levels.

In addition to state schools, there are privately-run schools (known as independent or public schools) that charge tuition. In these schools, pupils benefit from small classes and a competitive system geared toward university entrance. These schools often have more funds than state schools for extracurricular activities such as sports, drama, and music. There are around 2,500 independent schools in the UK, with some 615,000 children enrolled —about 7 percent of all British children, and 18 percent of students over age sixteen. Some religious groups also run schools, with an emphasis on their faith's values and teachings.

The A Level examinations or their equivalent are needed to enter a university in Britain. Most undergraduate schools are state-financed, which helps keep higher education somewhat affordable. The average tuition in 2014 was £9,000 ($14,000) per academic year. The government is trying to encourage more students to attend university. In 2013, one study reported that a record high level of 49 percent of students in England was "likely to go on to higher education," but some researchers challenge those findings as misleadingly high. Though the figures are difficult to pin down, it seems that the majority of UK students do not go on to college, but growing numbers do.

University students protest against an increase in tuition fees in Newcastle, England.

HEALTH CARE

Basic health care is provided free of charge by the National Health Service (NHS), funded with tax revenues by the central government. The service, with its rising costs and rising expectations, is a constant subject of political debate, but is nevertheless considered one of Britain's greatest policy successes. Primarily funded through the general taxation system, the system provides health care to every legal resident in the United Kingdom, with most services free at the point of use.

Today the NHS is challenged by, among other concerns, the growing proportion of elderly people in the population. The UK government predicts that by 2051, one-quarter of all citizens will be over sixty-five, and 7 percent will be over the age of eighty-five. Britons worry that the increased health needs for such a large elderly population will be enormously expensive and will strain the system.

INTERNET LINKS

www.royal.gov.uk
The official website of the British monarchy is full of news, information, and images of the royal family.

www.prosperity.com
The Legatum Prosperity Index is explained in more detail on this website.

www.nhs.uk/NHSEngland/thenhs/about/Pages/overview.aspx
The official site of the National Health Service has an informative overview.

www.gov.uk/government/organisations/department-for-education
The UK Department for Education website has news and statistics.

RELIGION

A little girl stands by an ancient Celtic Cross in Wales.

8

GREAT BRITAIN IS OFFICIALLY A Christian country, but not all belong to the Anglican Church, nor are they all Christians. About 60 percent of the English are Christian, and 40 percent belong to the Church of England. Of these, about three out of ten people attend Sunday services regularly, but more attend on holidays or in times of personal need. Many people value their local church community and the work it does, even if they are not a part of it.

Times have changed since the days of Henry VIII, when it was mandatory for all to follow the Christian denomination determined by the monarch. The religious face of the British population has grown far more diverse in the last century than it used to be when the main question was, "Are we Catholic or Protestant?" Today, the UK is a place of many people with many faiths.

CHRISTIANITY

Many denominations of Christianity are found in Britain, all with their own followers. England and Scotland each has its own official church, but the Scottish church is not a state church like England's. One in five Christians is aged sixty-five or over.

According to the 2011 UK census, the majority of residents identify as Christian, followed by Islam, Hinduism, Sikhism, Judaism, and Buddhism. Muslims tend to be younger and the most ethnically diverse. Christians tend to be older, while Hindus are the most likely not to be born in the United Kingdom. Twenty-three percent of Britons follow no religion.

Westminster Abbey in London was the location of the wedding of Prince William and Kate Middleton in 2011.

THE CHURCH OF ENGLAND   This is the Anglican Church created by Henry VIII in 1533 when he (and by extension all of England) broke away from the Roman Catholic Church. Today the prime minister makes most senior appointments in the church, in consultation with church leaders. The monarch is the nominal head of the church, and Parliament has a voice in its rituals. The monarch's title is "Defender of the Faith," but Prince Charles has said that he would like to change it to "Defender of Faiths" when he becomes king, to more fully reflect British society in the twenty-first century.

The Church of England is one of Britain's major landowners. Rents and income from land are administered by the Church Commission and are used to pay clerical salaries and the costs of maintaining its many church buildings. Extensive renovations, increasingly necessary for many cathedrals and churches, are generally funded by local or nationwide charity appeals.

The Church of England is divided into two administrative provinces, Canterbury and York, each of which has an archbishop. Beneath them are forty-four dioceses, each with a bishop. These in turn are divided into over thirteen thousand individual parishes.

The 467 members of the General Synod, the church's law-making body, decide overall matters of policy by discussion and voting. For instance, in 1992, the synod voted to approve the ordination of women as priests. Until 2015, however, women were not able to hold the top offices in the church, a divisive policy that caused much debate among members. In autumn 2014, the General Synod voted to amend church laws to allow the appointment of female bishops.

Church of England bishops speak out on matters of social policy; international and political affairs; marriage and family issues; health, environmental, and ethical concerns; and many other aspects of life in England.

THE CHURCH OF SCOTLAND As part of the 1707 Act of Union with England and Wales, Scotland was allowed to keep its own church. The Church of Scotland, known informally as the Kirk—its Scots language name—was founded in 1560 by the strict Calvinist John Knox. The church developed into a staunchly Presbyterian organization and remains completely separate from the Church of England as well as from the government. The Scottish Episcopal Church is Scotland's Anglican church.

Saint Conan's Kirk in Scotland

The Kirk claims about 400,000 members, which is a mere 7.5 percent of the population, but in the 2011 census, 32 percent of Scots claimed some affiliation. The membership is aging, however, which does not bode well for a robust church membership in the future. In addition, issues relating to homosexuality, such as the ordination of gay ministers and the acceptance of gay marriage, have caused great division among the church membership. The number of people who attend church varies widely by region, and a majority do not. Traditional Sunday practices, such as non-consumption of alcohol in pubs and abstaining from fishing and sports, are no longer strictly observed.

The church of Saint Tudno, built in the twelfth century, is in the north of Wales.

WALES There is an autonomous Anglican church, the Church in Wales, with six dioceses under a single province, with about 75,000 members. In 2020, the Church in Wales will celebrate its centenary, and has established a "2020 Vision" program for the years leading up to it.

The bulk of Welsh Christians are Nonconformist or Methodist, followers of the eighteenth-century evangelist John Wesley. His message of hard work and thrift appealed to the growing working classes of the time.

OTHER PROTESTANT SECTS The Methodist community in Britain is not confined to Wales. A total of 450,000 adult members and a community of 1.3 million is spread across Britain, concentrated predominantly in the old industrial working-class areas. It is one of what are known as the Free Churches, those which reject Episcopal rule and hierarchical structures, concentrating instead on local leadership. The strictest Methodists abstain from all alcohol.

Other sects include the Baptists and the United Reformed Church, a melding of the Congregational Church of England and Wales and the Presbyterian Church of England. The Religious Society of Friends, or Quakers, is known for its pacifist views. Smaller sects include the Unitarians, Jehovah's Witnesses, Seventh Day Adventists, Christian Scientists, Spiritualists, and the Salvation Army, which is best known for its brass bands playing carols and anthems in order to raise money for projects for the poor and destitute.

ROMAN CATHOLICISM There are roughly five million Roman Catholics in Britain, partly the result of Irish and Polish immigrants, and about half are active church members. The Cardinal Archbishop of Westminster is the senior

The Bristol Cathedral Choir performs traditional Christmas carols in the Cabot Circus shopping mall.

prelate, and the senior lay Catholic is the Duke of Norfolk. Britain has seven Catholic provinces: four in England, one in Wales, and two in Scotland, each with an archbishop, and below them are thirty dioceses and three thousand parishes. There are large Catholic communities in Liverpool and Glasgow, cities with large Irish immigrant communities. Elsewhere, local pockets of Catholicism sometimes date back to the days of persecution in the sixteenth century.

Historically, Catholics have been seen as politically suspect, owing allegiance to the pope in Rome as opposed to the monarch of England. There were Catholic plots against Elizabeth I and James I, and Catholic support for Bonnie Prince Charlie in the eighteenth century. Even in the twenty-first century, it would not be possible for a monarch or heir to the throne to marry a Roman Catholic without a major constitutional change.

OTHER RELIGIONS

ISLAM Britain's approximately 3.3 million Muslims make up the second-largest religious group after Christianity. It is also the fastest growing religion,

with around 100,000 converts reported in the 2011 census. The majority of British Muslims are of the Sunni denomination, and the largest single ethnic group, at 38 percent, are Pakistani immigrants and their descendents. Other Muslims come from Bangladesh and other South Asian countries; Arab countries such as Yemen, Syria, Iraq, Lebanon, Jordan, and Palestine; and African countries such as Nigeria and Somalia.

British protesters hold up a banner opposing Islamic dress during a march and rally in Exeter, Devon.

The integration of Muslims into British culture has not gone smoothly. Muslims tend to hold very strong conservative views—particularly regarding marriage, family, and sexuality issues—that are sometimes at odds with contemporary British society. Radical Islam, while not indicative of the majority of Muslims, is a problem that is forcing Britain to confront the conflicts between free speech and tolerance and what many regard as the inflammatory hate speech preached by a minority of Muslim leaders. On the other hand, British Muslims complain that they are the targets of discrimination, attacks, and negative stereotyping.

JUDAISM Britain's Jewish community is the second largest in Europe, with more than 263,000 members and 409 synagogues. Most are Ashkenazim Jews (from Germany and central Europe), with a small number of Sephardim (from Spain, Portugal, and North Africa). The majority are Orthodox Jews, and their chief spokesman is the Chief Rabbi, while there are smaller numbers of Reform Jews, Liberal Jews, and Strictly Orthodox. Roughly two in three Jewish children attend Jewish denominational schools.

Most British people find anti-Semitism to be repugnant and unacceptable in modern society. But the large, fast influx of Muslim (particularly Arab) immigrants has caused a surge in anti-Jewish incidents in the twenty-first century, as passions fuelled by the problem of Israel and the Palestinians play out on the streets of London and other cities.

OTHER GROUPS Chinese communities in London and other big cities mainly practice Buddhism. There are also Sikhs and Hindus and other Asian religious groups. However, a growing number of people do not subscribe to any particular faith and classify themselves as atheist, agnostic, or humanist.

Central Synagogue, an Orthodox Jewish temple, in Birmingham in the West Midlands of England

INTERNET LINKS

www.churchofengland.org
The Church of England website explains its beliefs, rituals, and views, as well as key facts and statistics.

www.churchofscotland.org.uk
The Church of Scotland website explains the church doctrine, laws and traditions, and news.

www.churchinwales.org.uk
The Church in Wales website covers issues and news relating to this Anglican Church.

www.isb.org.uk
The site of the Islamic Society of Britain offers information and news in English.

LANGUAGE

A refugee from Burundi studies the English language in a school in Kent, England.

9

THE ENGLISH LANGUAGE IS THE third-most-common native language in the world, after Mandarin and Spanish, with approximately 335 million native speakers. However, it is the most popular second language in the world, which adds another 505 million speakers. English is the principal language in the United Kingdom, the Republic of Ireland, the United States, Canada, Australia, New Zealand, the Bahamas, Jamaica, Grenada, Trinidad and Tobago, and Guyana. It is also the official language of several African countries, and is used widely as a language of commerce throughout the world. It is one of the six official languages of the United Nations, and one of the two official languages of the Olympics.

Many words are spelled differently in British English and American English. For example, *humour*, *centre*, and *plough* are British spellings, while *humor*, *center*, and *plow* are American. In 1829, when the American Noah Webster published a dictionary of American English, he created new spellings that he thought made more sense. Other changes came about through usage.

The pronunciation, usage, vocabulary, and syntax used in different English-speaking countries vary greatly. Just like any other language, English is constantly changing and developing. There are new words for new concepts being added and words falling into disuse or taking different meanings as circumstances change.

THE DEVELOPMENT OF THE ENGLISH LANGUAGE

When the Romans invaded Britain in 43 CE, the indigenous people spoke a Celtic language. Under the Romans, Latin was the preferred tongue among administrators and upper classes, but it did not filter down to the common people.

English in its oldest form was brought to Britain by invading Germanic groups from the fifth century onward, who pushed the Celts to the outlying mountainous areas of Wales and Cornwall. The word *English* comes from one of these groups, the Angles, who came from what is now Denmark.

OLD ENGLISH

The language as it was spoken between 450 and 1150 is called Old English. Four kingdoms existed from the fifth to the eighth centuries—Northumbria, Mercia, Kent, and West Saxony (Wessex)—each with their own language variations. By the tenth century, the West Saxon language became the official language, and most Old English manuscripts were transcribed in that area of the country. *Beowulf*, a 3,000-line epic poem, (first lines shown below) is the greatest surviving example of the literature and language of this period.

Old English	Modern English
Hwæt we Gardena ingear dagum, þeod cyninga þrym ge frunon huða æþelingas ellen fremedon.	Lo! We spear-armed Danes in days of old heard the glory of the tribal kings, how the princes did courageous deeds.

Old English is barely recognizable as English. Like other Germanic languages, its nouns had cases and genders. The language was originally written in a series of straight lines called runes, which were easy to inscribe on stone or wood. Christian missionaries who arrived in Britain starting in 597 brought the Roman alphabet, which was widely adopted. As Christianity spread, with Latin used in church services, hundreds of Latin words crept into the English language. These include *bishop*, *abbot*, *candle*, and *angel*. The Viking invaders of the tenth and eleventh centuries added various Scandinavian or Old Norse words to the language, such as *fog*, *skull* (*skulle* = "head"), *egg*, and *sky* ("cloud").

The Norman invasion in 1066 had a huge impact on the English language, bringing thousands of French terms into everyday use. For nearly 150 years, the new nobility and most of the church hierarchy were French-speaking Normans. Many of the French words were additions, rather than replacements, so that English now, for example, has not only *chicken* and *cow* but the French-derived *poultry* and *beef*. These additions account for the rich vocabulary of today's English.

The fourteenth-century English poet Geoffrey Chaucer is pictured on a horse in the Ellesmere manuscript of his *Canterbury Tales.*

MIDDLE ENGLISH

The language evolved to a form called Middle English between approximately 1150 and 1500. Beginning in the late fourteenth century, English—rather than the previously preferred French—was taught in schools and used in law courts. Prior to that, English had been thought too coarse or common a language for important uses. King Henry IV (1399—1413) was the first king whose primary language was English. By the early fourteenth century, the dialect of London had become a recognized standard as exemplified in the works of Geoffrey Chaucer. The opening lines of *The Canterbury Tales* provide an example of what Middle English looked like. (See next page.)

Middle English	Modern English (rough translation)
Whan that Aprille with his shoures sote The droghte of Marche hath perced to the rote, And bathed every veyne in swich licour,	When April with its sweet-smelling showers Has pierced the drought of March to the root And bathed every vein in such liquor (or liquid)
Of which vertu engendred is the flour ...	By which virtue generates the flower...

MODERN ENGLISH

In 1450, the language began to undergo a dramatic change in pronunciation called The Great Vowel Shift. One change was that people stopped pronouncing the final *e* on words. For example, the word *made* had been pronounced "mah-duh." Spelling was just beginning to be standardized around this same time, which explains some of the peculiarities of English spelling, with oddities such as silent letters. At one time, those letters were pronounced.

By the time William Shakespeare wrote his famous works around the year 1600, the language had taken a form now called Early Modern English. From that to today's English was a progression of just a few centuries, during which time many more people learned to read, were able to travel abroad—thus spreading the language far and wide—and finally, were able access the English language through new technologies.

THE WELSH LANGUAGE (*CYMRAEG*)

Around 20 percent of the population of Wales can speak Welsh, one of the Celtic languages, but many more understand it. Road signs and town names are bilingual in Welsh and English.

Welsh is a phonetic language similar to French Breton and the Cornish language, which died out in the eighteenth century. The letters *j, k, q, v, x,* and *z* do not appear in Welsh. *W* and *i* can be both vowel and consonant, with different sounds for each. *Y* is used as a vowel, pronounced "uh." *Ch* is a guttural sound, as in the Scottish *loch*; *f* is pronounced "v"; *ff* renders the English "f" sound; *dd* is pronounced as "th"; and *ll* roughly as "thl." A few common terms are *dydd da* (thuhd-dar), meaning "good day"; *sutmae* (soot-may), "how are you"; and *croeso* (kro-wee-so), "welcome."

A bilingual road sign in Welsh and English.

GAELIC AND SCOTS

Only about 57,000 people in Scotland speak Scottish Gaelic, and they are found mostly in the Highlands and Outer Hebrides. Like Welsh, Gaelic is a Celtic language, brought from Ireland to Scotland during the fifth century.

A road sign near Uig, Scotland, is written in both Gaelic and English.

Unlike Welsh, the language has no official status in Scotland but has been classified as an indigenous language. Gaelic words now used widely in English include *bard*, *glen*, *bog*, *slogan*, *whiskey*, *brogue*, *clan*, and *loch*. Scottish Gaelic is different from Irish Gaelic and is also different from Scots, an ancient variety of English with its own distinct dialects. Most Scots speakers live in the Scottish Lowlands.

ENGLISH DIALECTS AND ACCENTS

The way a person speaks is a good indication of where he or she comes from. A Welsh person speaks English with a musical, singsong lilt, while a Scottish person has a pronounced, almost guttural accent. Those who come from the West Country widen vowels and pronounce "s" as "z," so that "cider" becomes "zoyder." Midlands accents in the Birmingham area are flatter and more nasal.

Many of these local variations are the result of centuries of regional developments in the English language. For example, in a wide area north of the Humber River, across Yorkshire and over the border to Scotland, people still say "lang" rather than "long." In an area stretching farther south into Derbyshire and Nottinghamshire, words such as "night," "right," and "fright" are pronounced with an "ee" sound as in "neat." The southern pronunciation of a long "ah" in "past," "path," and "laugh" never progressed beyond a diagonal line from the Wash in East Anglia to Wales; north of that line people tend to use a short "a" as in "flat" for these words.

Together with the age-old local dialects, Britain's immigrant population has brought further diversity and richness to English usage. For example, reggae and rap music generally feature in the rich English patois of the West Indian population.

Standard English, sometimes called the King's or Queen's English, or Received Pronunciation, is the pronunciation generally used by educated people of the middle and upper classes, and by most announcers on BBC radio and television. The richness and variety of pronunciation and accents is a major component of the renowned British sense of humor.

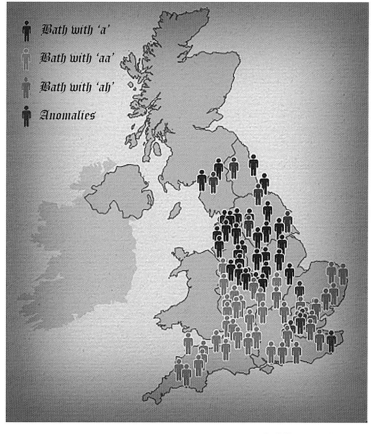

Bath with 'a'

Bath with 'aa'

Bath with 'ah'

Anomalies

A difference in British accents in the north and south: those in the north generally pronounce words such as *bath*, *grass*, and *dance* with a short vowel, like the "a" in the word *cat*, while those in the south use an "ah" sound.

INTERNET LINKS

www.englishclub.com/english-language-history.htm
This "History of the English Language" is a quick overview with a map and timeline.

www.thehistoryofenglish.com/index.html
This is an entertaining, informative, and much more in-depth history of English.

www.gaelicmatters.com/celtic-language.html
"The Celtic Language—the basics and what it sounds like" covers the varieties of Celtic languages in the British Isles.

ARTS

"Rain, Steam, and Speed —The Great Western Railway" (1844), a painting by J.M.W. Turner, depicts an early locomotive crossing the River Thames. the painting depicts an early locomotive of the Great Western Railway crossing the River Thames.

10

G REAT BRITAIN HAS LONG BEEN A vibrant source of the arts—from ancient objects in stone, tin, and gold to the latest, cutting-edge digital media. The island's contribution to the world's art scene is out of proportion to its small size—it's a key center of the global art world. Britain's artistic heritage is world renowned, from the plays of William Shakespeare and the paintings of John Constable to the music of The Beatles and beyond.

CLASSICAL MUSIC

EARLY MUSIC AND THE BAROQUE Early English music was mainly written for the Catholic Church. Thomas Tallis (1505—1585), under Henry VIII, composed music for the new Anglican Church, while his pupil William Byrd wrote numerous madrigals, choral works, and string and keyboard works. In the seventeenth century, Henry Purcell (1659—1695) wrote church music and harpsichord pieces, as well as the operas *Dido and Aeneas* and *The Indian Queen*, all of which combined the older medieval tones and scales of the English tradition with Italian and French styles. George Friedrich Handel (1685—1759), under the patronage of

"The world is wide, no two days are alike, nor even two hours; neither were there ever two leaves of a tree alike since the creation of all the world; and the genuine productions of art, like those of nature, are all distinct from each other."
—John Constable (1776—1837), English landscape painter

King George I, composed *Music for the Royal Fireworks*, *Water Music*, and *The Messiah*. These works are still played and enjoyed today.

NINETEENTH CENTURY AND BEYOND Late nineteenth-century composers include Arthur Sullivan (1842—1900), who teamed up with his contemporary W. S. Gilbert to compose fourteen Gilbert and Sullivan operettas, including *H.M.S. Pinafore*, *The Pirates of Penzance*, and *The Mikado*. Edward Elgar (1857—1934) is famed for his *Enigma Variations*, his haunting *Cello Concerto*, and the "Pomp and Circumstance" marches, which echoed the self-assurance of colonial Britain. Ralph Vaughan Williams (1872—1958) was inspired by the rediscovery of English folk songs and featured them in such works as *Fantasia on Greensleeves*.

POPULAR MUSIC

Genres originating in Great Britain, or radically influenced by British musicians, include a broad range of rock music. Two bands led British popular music onto the world stage in the 1960s—The Beatles and The Rolling Stones. The Beatles, a quartet from Liverpool, had their first hit in 1962 with

The Beatles perform on stage at the London Palladium in front of 2,000 screaming fans.

"Love Me Do" and dominated the British pop music scene until they split up in 1970. They made their grand entrance into the US market with a historic appearance on *The Ed Sullivan Show* in 1964 that was seen by more than 70 million viewers. They are widely regarded as the greatest pop group in history and remain as an iconic musical influence on many of today's bands. The Rolling Stones released "Satisfaction" in 1965, one of many hit singles and albums spanning the next four decades. The legendary rockers have been inducted in the Rock and Roll Hall of Fame.

The 1970s saw the emergence of colorful individual artists such as Elton John and David Bowie and a division between teenagers and older rock fans. Meanwhile, the punk rock movement tried to reclaim rock music for the young and rebellious. Groups such as The Sex Pistols and The Clash shocked people with their rude behavior and outrageous appearance. In the 1980s came synthesizer rock and bands such as The Eurythmics and the iconic group Queen. The band The Police launched the solo career of its lead singer and bassist, Sting, who has also become an activist for social justice issues around the world. One of the biggest pop groups in the 1990s was the Spice Girls, who were equally known for their raunchy music videos. Rap, hip hop, or Brit-hop, also took off in the 1990s and evolved into a wide variety of urban music genres. The twenty-first century has seen British soul singers Amy Winehouse, Joss Stone, and Adele top the charts.

British singer Adele arrives at the Oscars ceremony in Hollywood in 2013.

LITERATURE

The breadth and richness of British poetry, prose, and drama stretch over ten centuries.

POETRY In the fourteenth century, the British poet Geoffrey Chaucer published *The Canterbury Tales*, a collection of stories about a group of pilgrims on a journey to visit a religious shrine at Canterbury Cathedral.

BESIDE THE LAKE, BENEATH THE TREES

The scenic beauty of the Lake District inspired a group of nineteenth-century English poets, who came to be called the Lake Poets. William Wordsworth, one of the best-known poets of the English Romantic movement, was born in the region.

One day in April 1802, Wordsworth and his sister Dorothy were walking along the shore of Ullswater, the second largest lake in the Lake District, when they came upon a mass of daffodils. The sight inspired him to write what has become one of the world's most famous poems.

I WANDERED LONELY AS A CLOUD
By William Wordsworth (1804)

I wandered lonely as a cloud
That floats on high o'er vales and hills,
When all at once I saw a crowd,
A host of golden daffodils;
Beside the lake, beneath the trees,
Fluttering and dancing in the breeze.

Continuous as the stars that shine
And twinkle on the milky way,
They stretched in never-ending line
Along the margin of a bay:
Ten thousand saw I at a glance,
Tossing their heads in sprightly dance.

The waves beside them danced; but they
Out-did the sparkling waves in glee:
A poet could not but be gay,
In such a jocund company:
I gazed—and gazed—but little thought
What wealth the show to me had brought:

For oft, when on my couch I lie
In vacant or in pensive mood,
They flash upon that inward eye
Which is the bliss of solitude;
And then my heart with pleasure fills,
And dances with the daffodils.

KING ARTHUR, MYTH OR LEGEND?

One of Britain's most enduring heroes is King Arthur. Legend has it that he was a great Celtic leader of the late fifth and early sixth century, who defended Britain against the invading Saxons. No one knows if Arthur was a real person or entirely fictional; the debate is ongoing and passionate.

Many ancient tales from various sources mention Arthur, but there is no one definitive story. Nevertheless, over the centuries, certain storytellers have elaborated on these legends to create a great body of fantastical and romantic literature called Arthurian Legends. The earliest known works about Arthur include History of the Kings of Britain, *c.1138, by the Welsh monk Geoffrey of Monmouth; the works of the twelfth century French poet Chrétien de Troyes; and Sir Thomas Malory's compilation of traditional tales,* Le Morte d'Arthur *("The Death of Arthur"), first published in 1485. These are the stories of Camelot, Arthur's peaceable kingdom: his magical sword Excalibur, his wife Queen Guinevere, Sir Lancelot, Merlin the Magician, the Knights of the Round Table, and a host of other characters.*

Modern writers continue to explore the Arthur stories. T. H. White's popular The Once and Future King, *first published in 1958, is a reinterpretation of the old texts. The Broadway musical* Camelot *was a smash hit in 1960 and was made into a movie in 1967. The idealistic administration of US president John F. Kennedy was sometimes called "Camelot."*

But King Arthur and his Camelot are first and foremost symbols of Great Britain—myth masquerading as a glorious history, and in the process, embodying the essence of what makes Great Britain what it is.

The greatest British literary phenomenon of the twentieth to twenty-first centuries is the Harry Potter fantasy series by the English writer J. K. Rowling. An unemployed, single mother when she began writing, Rowling became a multi-millionaire within five years of the release of the first book Harry Potter and the Philosopher's Stone *in 1997. In total, she wrote seven books in the series and today Rowling is the best-selling living author in the United Kingdom, with sales exceeding four hundred million copies. Although the books are categorized as children's books, many adults read them as well.*

Harry Potter, the series' protagonist, is an orphan boy who discovers he is a wizard.

He attends an exclusive school of wizardry where he learns the magical arts, and not incidentally, grows up along the way. Throughout the series, Harry's quest is to overcome the Dark wizard Lord Voldemort, in a classic story of good conquering evil.

In addition to being the best-selling book series in history, the Harry Potter books were made into an eight-part film series. It became the highest-grossing film series in history.

The *Tales* was the first piece of English literature written in the vernacular, that is, the everyday language of the people—which in this case was Middle English—rather than in Latin or French, which were considered superior languages. Chaucer therefore is often heralded as the "Father of English Literature."

John Milton's seventeenth-century epic poem *Paradise Lost*, based on biblical references, conjures vivid images of Adam and Eve, Hell, and Satan's fall from Heaven. John Donne, who also lived in the seventeenth century, was a metaphysical poet who used wit and clever puns to convey complex ideas.

William Shakespeare is so revered as a poet and playwright that he is known as "The Bard"—not a bard, but the Bard with a capital B. Between 1588 and 1613, he wrote thirty-seven plays, more than 150 sonnets, and numerous poems. The Royal Shakespeare Company, founded in 1879, has two theaters devoted to his works: the Swan Theatre in Stratford-on-Avon, his town of birth; and the Globe Theatre in London. While the language can be a bit hard to understand, the verse is rich, complex, clever and sometimes hilarious, and the themes and characters are vibrant and relevant four centuries later.

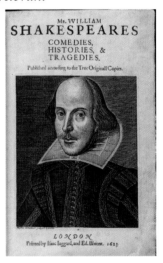

His historical plays are narratives of the lives of certain English kings. His comedies are generally lighthearted tales of love, with many a twist and turn before a happy ending. But Shakespeare's crowning glories are his tragedies. Romeo and Juliet, *one of his most popular plays, is a story of star-crossed young lovers. In the plays* Macbeth, Othello, Hamlet, *and* King Lear, *the central tragic hero is dominated by a fierce emotion or character flaw that leads to his eventual downfall: ambition in* Macbeth, *jealousy in* Othello, *revenge and indecision in* Hamlet, *and pride in* King Lear.

The eighteenth-century Scottish poet Robert Burns used his local dialect to describe Scottish scenery and customs in poems such as "Tam O'Shanter" and in songs such as "Auld Lang Syne." Of the late eighteenth-century and early nineteenth-century poets, William Wordsworth's lyrical poetry about the Lake District and John Keats's romantic descriptive verse on the beauties of nature are well known.

Early twentieth-century war poets Rupert Brooke, Siegfried Sassoon, and Wilfred Owen all describe the horror of the trench warfare of World War I. The Welsh poet Dylan Thomas captivated the lilting musical quality of English spoken by Welsh people; the radio play *Under Milk Wood* is one of his more famous works. Britain has an official poet laureate, appointed by the monarch to write official poetry on state occasions. Since 2009, the Scottish poet Carol Ann Duffy has held the position.

PROSE Writers include Samuel Johnson (eighteenth century), who wrote essays on issues of contemporary interest, and Sir Winston Churchill (twentieth century), who wrote *History of the English-Speaking Peoples*, a four-volume history of Britain from Roman times until Queen Victoria's reign.

Novels became popular during the nineteenth century, with carefully crafted social observations by Jane Austen, romantic tales by Charlotte Brontë, gritty urban realism from Charles Dickens, and tragic rural stories from Thomas Hardy. Twentieth-century novels include satires by Evelyn Waugh, tales of the sea from Joseph Conrad, working-class sensuality from D.H. Lawrence, and Graham Greene's movie-like narrative techniques.

Children's literature is forever richer thanks to Beatrix Potter's Peter Rabbit series, J. M. Barrie's *Peter Pan*, Robert Louis Stevenson's *Treasure Island*, Lewis Carroll's Alice in Wonderland books, A. A. Milne's Winnie-the-Pooh books, and P. L. Travers's *Mary Poppins*.

Prestigious literary prizes are awarded annually for original works of fiction, generating widespread interest in new writing. Novelists such as Helen Oyeyemi, Hilary Mantel, Neil Gaiman, David Mitchell, and Ian McEwan are just a few of the many notable British writers of today.

FILM AND TELEVISION

Britain's film industry is world class, and at the top of that class as well. Some of the top movies of the twenty-first century include *Slumdog Millioniare*, by English film director Danny Boyle in 2008, and *12 Years a Slave*, by English director Steve McQueen in 2013, both of which won an Academy Award for Best Picture.

One particularly enduring British film icon is the character James Bond, a fictional secret agent created by novelist Ian Fleming in 1953. There are twenty-six James Bond movies, from *Dr. No* in 1962 to *Spectre*, planned for a 2015 release, in which seven actors have played Bond.

In 2010, the television drama series *Downton Abbey*, starring the talented English actress Maggie Smith, became the latest in a long tradition of British TV phenomena to wow audiences not only in Britain but Canada and the United States as well. Britain also has a strong tradition of TV comedy, such as the classic Monty Python series. And just as in the United States, reality TV programs became popular in the 2000s. The hit singing talent search program *Pop Idol*, created by the English producer Simon Fuller, ran from 2001 to 2003, but spawned similar shows worldwide, including the much longer-running *American Idol*.

Actors and workers are on the set of *Downton Abbey* in Newbury, England.

ART AND ARCHITECTURE

In the sixteenth century, the Protestant Reformation put an end to a great deal of visual art in England. Public works of religious imagery, such as paintings and sculptures, were considered to be idolatry, and were associated with Roman Catholicism. At that time, most artwork was religious in nature, so the effect on the art world was chilling. Many existing artworks were destroyed.

The painting tradition, once it began to recover from the effects of the Reformation, focused mainly on portraiture and landscapes. Wealthy patrons imported portrait painters from Europe, but British landscape painting rose into its own. J.M.W. Turner (1775—1851), an English painter, transformed the landscape genre. This "painter of light" expressed the sublime power of nature by focusing on the effects of color and radiance in the composition rather than on detail, a controversial approach at the time. John Constable (1776—1837),

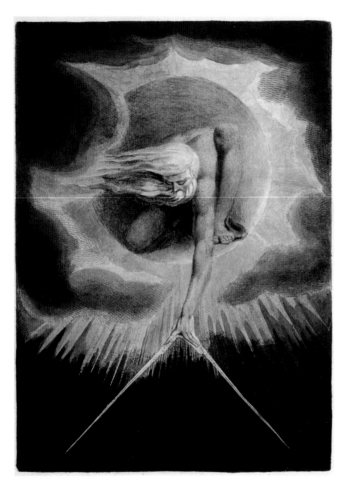

"The Ancient of Days" is a painting by William Blake.

another English landscape artist, painted images of real English landscapes rather than the imaginary scenes that were the custom.

One English painter (and poet) who defies categorization is William Blake (1757–1827). His visionary works, which include religious subject matter, have emotional, psychological, and hallucinatory qualities that were so revolutionary that they were mostly rejected during his lifetime. It wasn't until the twentieth century that his work found an enthusiastic audience.

Britain's rich architectural heritage is highly varied, stretching back over ten centuries of religious, civic, business, and domestic styles. The Tower of London and Durham Cathedral are examples of eleventh-century Norman style. Exeter Cathedral shows the later Decorated style of English Gothic architecture (1350–1400), while King's College Chapel in Cambridge, built in 1446, is done in the Perpendicular style.

Inigo Jones in the early seventeenth century developed the Continental Palladian style in buildings such as the Queen's House in Greenwich. Sir Christopher Wren, a seventeenth-century architect, left a legacy of fifty-two city churches, including Saint Paul's Cathedral, which was built after the Fire of London in 1666, and another four churches outside the City of London.

The curving Georgian-style Royal Crescent in Bath was designed by John Wood the Younger around 1775. The whole city is an architectural delight. Edinburgh's New Town is another example of the same architectural style. Robert Adam's Classical style is typified by Syon House in Middlesex. Striking examples of Victorian architecture remain in Sir George Gilbert Scott's Saint Pancras Railway Station and Albert Memorial. The Houses of Parliament, by

Charles Barry, is also a fine example of Victorian design.

Modern buildings in London continue the tradition of phenomenal British architecture. The Swiss Re building, commonly known as "The Gherkin," is a spiral skyscraper built in 2003 by Norman Foster and Partners. The London Eye, a giant Ferris wheel on the South Bank of the River Thames in London; the Millennium Bridge, a suspended footbridge over the same river; and the Millennium Dome in Greenwich, a huge indoor arena, were all built to usher in the twenty-first century.

"The Gherkin" building in London was awarded a Royal Institute of British Architects Stirling Prize in 2004.

INTERNET LINKS

www.bbc.co.uk/history/ancient/anglo_saxons/arthur_01.shtml
"King Arthur, 'Once and Future King," is a quick overview of the Arthurian Legends and what they mean to Britain.

www.jkrowling.com
Author J. K. Rowling's official site provides news about her philanthropy, charities, and other projects, as well as literary news.

www.bbc.co.uk/history/people/william_shakespeare
The BBC's History site has a section devoted to The Bard.

www.rollingstone.com/music/artists/the-beatles
Rolling Stone magazine's site presents an excellent section on The Beatles, with timelines, pictures, videos, bios, and more.

LEISURE

A young boy plays with a toy boat at Hope Cove Beach in Devon, England.

THE BRITISH SPEND THEIR DOWN time in much the same way people do in most Western countries: listening to music, watching TV, shopping, visiting with friends and family, or playing video games. Kids and teens play sports, take lessons, hang out, or catch up on their homework.

Some people spend their weekends tinkering with motorcycles and cars, repairing or working on their vehicles in the garage and backyard; others have different hobbies. Fishing is by far the national pastime. Fishing spots range from canals and reservoirs to rivers where Scottish salmon can be caught.

SPORTS

Sir Winston Churchill's comment in 1938 that sports was "the first of all the British amusements" rings true even today. Sports are an integral part of the British way of life: millions of viewers watch soccer, rugby, cricket, and horse racing on television every weekend. Participation in sports is also popular. At school, children are encouraged to take part in games of soccer or rugby (for boys), hockey, netball and lacrosse, and cricket, athletics, running, swimming, or tennis in summer. Schools compete in numerous local leagues, as do towns, counties, clubs, pubs, and companies.

In 2012 London hosted the Olympic Summer Games, which featured twenty-six sports including water events, equestrian events,

11

One of the most popular and longest-running TV shows in Britain is the sci-fi classic Dr. Who. The show, which originally began in 1963 and ran until 1989, follows the adventures of a time- and space-traveling Time Lord, or humanoid alien called "The Doctor." The series was relaunched in 2005 and continues to be broadcast in more than fifty countries.

gymnastics, track, cycling, wrestling, and more. At the end of the weeks of competition, British athletes took home sixty-five medals, the third-highest medal count, bested only by the United States, with 104 medals, and China, with eighty-eight.

FOOTBALL Soccer, called football in Britain (and most everywhere outside of the United States), is the most widely followed sport, with national and international matches televised several times a week. English football is organized into two principal annual competitions: the League Championship and the Football Association (FA) Cup. The former is divided into four divisions: the Premier League and Divisions One, Two, and Three. Teams score three points for a victory and one point for a tie. The team with the most points at the end of the season wins the championship. At the end of each season, the bottom three teams in each division move down a division, while the top two teams in each division move up. A play-off competition between the next top four teams decides the third team to move up a division. The last team in Division Three is relegated to a minor league.

The FA Cup is a knockout competition where teams must win matches to stay in the competition. There are separate Welsh and Scottish soccer leagues. England, Scotland, and Wales also take part in the European Championship once every four years. Individual teams can take part in various European competitions if they qualify, while the national teams take part in the World Cup held every four years.

Soccer is occasionally accompanied by incidents of "hooliganism," where supporters get out of control and sometimes become violent as a response to a bad decision made by the referee or an unexpected defeat. Such behavior is seen as more than simply bad sportsmanship, but as a sociological phenomenon linked to unemployment, poverty, and social discontent.

WINTER SPORTS The game of rugby was started at Rugby School in 1823. Rugby Union, traditionally an amateur game but now moving toward professionalism, has an annual series competition known as the Six Nations Championship played between England, Wales, Scotland, Ireland, Italy, and

Dean Schofield of London Welsh takes the ball during the European Rugby Challenge Cup match between London Welsh and Edinburgh Rugby in December 2014, in Oxford, England.

GARDENS

Gardening is a major hobby for many people. Many homes have a small plot of land, whether a suburban garden, an allotment at some distance from one's house or apartment, or a larger country garden. Newspapers have a regular column on gardening tips, and numerous gardening books line shelves of libraries and bookshops. A degree of competitiveness can take hold as neighbors try to outdo one another, especially during preparations for local horticultural shows.

More than 3,700 individual gardens are open to the public under the National Gardens Scheme, which raises money for charities. They include ordinary suburban gardens and those of large country houses. Examples of Elizabethan knot gardens, medieval walled enclosures of fruit trees, roses and herbs, well-tended mazes, eighteenth-century landscaped gardens, and cottage gardens with mixed vegetables and flowers abound throughout the country. Agricultural and horticultural shows are held throughout the summer months, and classes in gardening and flower arranging, which offer a wealth of ideas to the avid gardener, are available in the evenings.

France. Matches for this series, and for international test matches against rugby-playing countries such as Australia, New Zealand, and South Africa, are played on famous grounds: England's Twickenham, Scotland's Murrayfield, and Wales's Millennium Stadium. Rugby League, on the other hand, is a professional game and the players are paid. Each team has thirteen players instead of the fifteen in Rugby Union, and the rules differ slightly for tackling and in some other respects.

 Field hockey is played at many schools by both sexes. Lacrosse is played mainly by girls, while cross-country running is also quite popular.

SUMMER SPORTS During the summer, people play tennis and cricket, and running, swimming, and water sports are popular. Tennis clubs abound,

Cricket is popular among all age groups in Great Britain.

particularly in the southern counties. The All-England Championships have been held at Wimbledon since 1877.

Cricket is a game played by two teams of eleven players on a large field, using a red leather ball and a flat wooden bat. The teams bat and bowl alternately. Runs are scored by two batsmen running between the two wickets—three vertical sticks in the ground known as stumps, and two smaller sticks (bails) resting between them. The batsmen can be out of the game in a number of ways such as by fielding positions that limit the number of runs made and by bowling strategies that bowl the wickets down. The team scoring the most runs wins the game. Test matches (international games) can last for five days and still often end in a tie.

EQUINE SPORTS Horse racing takes place from the end of March to the first week of November. Races at Royal Ascot are noted for the hats worn by spectators as much as for the horse racing itself. The Queen and other members of the royal family often have their own horses running in the Royal Ascot races.

National Hunt races, over hurdles or larger fences, take place between February and June. The most important races are the Cheltenham Gold Cup and the Grand National at Aintree near Liverpool, which is the best-known steeplechase. Local hunts raise money and run their own point-to-point steeplechases during this period.

Competitions testing the riders' skill at cross-country, horsemanship, and jumping take place at Burghley and Badminton annually. Horse shows are held across Britain during the summer months, ranging from small village contests to the Royal Windsor Horse Show and the Royal International Horse Show at Hickstead in West Sussex.

OTHER OUTDOOR PURSUITS

Walking is extremely popular. Even in the pouring rain, groups of walkers clad in waterproof anoraks and boots, often accompanied by dogs, can be seen walking across fields and moors and along river banks. There are several long-distance footpaths, such as the Pennine Way that stretches for 268 miles (431 km) from the Peak District to the Scottish border. Footpaths, bridle paths for horseback riding, and tracks give walkers access to much of the countryside.

Rock climbing is popular in hilly areas such as around Mount Snowdon in Wales, Froggatt Edge in the Peak District, and numerous locations in the Lake District.

There is skiing in Scotland, although the snow can be unreliable. On a lesser scale, many families have toboggans to use on slopes in public parks and nearby fields in the winter. Many people skate on frozen ponds and rivers.

Sailing is popular, especially on the southern coast and on the Isle of Wight, where the Cowes Week Regatta takes place in early August. Tall ship races leave from Plymouth, Falmouth, and Southampton in July and August. Sailing, windsurfing, and water skiing take place on some reservoirs and lakes during the summer.

Children slide down a hill in Bramhall Park in Cheshire, England, after a winter snowfall.

INTERNET LINKS

www.olympic.org/london-2012-summer-olympics
Official site of the London 2012 Olympics shows highlights of the "happy and glorious" games.

www.ngs.org.uk
NGS Gardens Open for Charity is full of pictures of gardens throughout England.

www.bbc.com/sport
The BBC Sports section has up-to-the-minute news about a wide range of British sports.

FESTIVALS

A man runs carrying a tar-soaked burning barrel at a carnival in
Ottery St. Mary, England. The barrel run is a 400-year-old tradition.

12

THE CALENDAR IS CHOCK FULL of special days throughout Great Britain—religious, national, and secular. "Bank holidays" are official holidays, when most shops, schools, businesses, and government institutions are closed. There are numerous other, nonofficial days as well, such as Valentine's Day, Mother's Day, and Halloween.

Queen Elizabeth and her husband Prince Phillip don official robes for the Garter Day ceremonies at Windsor Castle.

A man dressed as a Viking takes part in the torchlight procession through Edinburgh for the start of the Hogmanay celebrations on December 30, 2013, in Scotland.

The year begins with the usual New Year's celebrations and with a touch of old tradition as well. In Scotland, New Year's Eve is called *Hogmanay*. This ancient holiday incorporates winter solstice customs that probably date back to pre-Christian times. One old ritual is the eating of haggis (spiced minced meat boiled in a sheep's stomach) before the "first footing." This custom, now rarely practiced, involves a tall man who visits homes bearing gifts and best wishes and tries to be the first foot in the door in the new year. There is the customary singing of "Auld Lang Syne," from a poem by the Scottish poet Robert Burns (1759—1796); and a few weeks later, on January 25, the man himself is celebrated. On Burns Night, revellers enjoy banquets, speeches, drinking, singing, recitations, and dancing.

In August, Wales puts on the National *Eisteddfod*, the country's biggest arts event and one of Europe's oldest cultural festivals. The nine-day festival celebrates Welsh music, literature, dance, and theater. Meanwhile, around the same time, the Edinburgh Festival Fringe—the world's largest arts festival—takes place in Scotland's capital.

November 5 is Guy Fawkes Day. Throughout England, bonfires are lit, old clothes are turned into effigies, and fireworks are set off to commemorate the failure of a plot in 1605 to blow up Parliament.

November 11 is Armistice Day, held to remember those who died in the two World Wars. The Queen, attended by political leaders, leads a procession of approximately a thousand veterans to lay wreaths at the Cenotaph, a war memorial in the Whitehall section of London. On that day, people wear red paper poppies in support of war veterans.

December 26 is Boxing Day. This day after Christmas is a bank holiday, and most people simply spend the day with their families, going for a walk, watching sports, or eating the Christmas leftovers. The holiday originated with the old custom of wealthy people giving a "Christmas box" of money or gifts to their servants and tradesmen.

NATIONAL DAYS Each of the British countries has its own National Day, based on the day of its patron saint. England's takes place on April 23, St. George's Day; Wales celebrates on March 1, St. David's Day; and Scotland observes November 30, St. Andrew's Day. Although none of these days are official bank holidays, many people across Britain are petitioning for their own country's day to be observed officially in that country.

RELIGIOUS FESTIVALS

Although Great Britain is made up of three Christian nations, they are religiously diverse nations as well. Naturally, they celebrate the Christian holidays, with Easter and Christmas being the most important of the year. Many nonreligious people, and some people of other religions celebrate a secular Christmas.

However, there are other religious holidays as well. The most important Jewish holidays are the autumn holidays of Rosh Hashanah, the Jewish New Year, and Yom Kippur, the Day of Atonement. Many British of Indian descent celebrate the Hindu holidays—such as Diwali, a colorful festival of light in the autumn. British Muslims celebrate the holy days of the Islamic calendar, with

Queen Elizabeth lays a wreath honoring veterans during the annual Remembrance Sunday Service at the Cenotaph on Whitehall on November 9, 2014, in London.

The British love of ceremony is best exemplified by the role of the royal family. Their daily appointments are listed in The Times's newspaper court circular column. There are various regular and customary occasions when the public can view royal pageantry.

The Changing of the Guard

• *The Changing of the Guard at Buckingham Palace takes place daily at 11:30 a.m. when the guards change shifts. The ceremony is very popular with tourists.*

• *The Trooping of the Colour is held on a Saturday in early June to celebrate the sovereign's official birthday. The queen, seated in a horse-drawn carriage, inspects the troops of her personal guard. This military ceremony dates to the early eighteenth century.*

• *The State Opening of Parliament occurs every November after the summer recess. The ceremony has scarcely changed since the sixteenth century. For this, the queen travels from Buckingham Palace in the Irish State Coach, and reads from the throne the Gracious Speech—a statement of the current government's legislative program for the coming year.*

• *Garter Day, an impressive ceremony at Windsor Castle held every June, is the day when new knights, chosen by the queen, are admitted into the Order of the Garter. It is the highest order of knighthood, and the oldest British Order of Chivalry, founded by Edward III in 1348.*

• *Queen Elizabeth II's Diamond Jubilee Year in 2012, marking her sixty years as queen, was filled with special celebrations throughout Great Britain and the Commonwealth.*

Eid-al-Fidr being one of the most important. This feast day marks the end of the month-long fasting holy month of Ramadan. Some Brits are petitioning the government to have Diwali and Eid declared official bank holidays, but so far Parliament has not approved the initiative.

COUNTRY FESTIVALS

Various regions celebrate rural festivities that date back over many centuries.

PLOUGH MONDAY In some areas, Plough Monday, the Monday after the Epiphany on January 6, is celebrated as the traditional resumption of plowing after the Twelve Days of Christmas celebrations have ended.

SUMMER SHOWS Appleby Horse Fair, a horse sale, is held every June in a picturesque village in the Lake District. A large proportion of villages and counties hold rural fêtes, shows, or contests during the summer months, generally for charity. Harvest festivals are held in churches throughout the country in late August, and churches are decorated with agricultural produce. In the West Country a Saxon custom of wassailing—wishing good health to the apple trees and cider drinkers—continues on January 17.

FOLK DANCE Morris dancing, a type of English folk dance based on the European Morisca, a Moorish dance, came to be associated with May Games, held on May 1, and with the characters from Robin Hood (as seen in the dancers' costumes). The dance is performed by men, usually accompanied by music from an accordion and drums, and is said to have derived from pagan fertility rites.

INTERNET LINKS

www.royal.gov.uk/RoyalEventsandCeremonies/Overview.aspx
The official site of the British monarchy has a section devoted to royal events and ceremonies.

www.educationuk.org/usa/articles/festivals-and-holidays
The British Council publishes this calendar of festivals, celebrations, and public holidays with many links to events.

FOOD

Celebrity chef Jamie Oliver joins schoolchildren in London to celebrate Food Revolution Day in May 2014.

13

ONCE UPON A TIME, NOT ALL THAT long ago, traditional British food had a reputation for being rather plain and bland. However, just as the English language has absorbed a broad range of words from other languages, so British cuisine has become more sophisticated, incorporating many global influences.

Today's typical British diet includes Italian-influenced dishes, such as pasta and pizza; American fast food, French cookery, Chinese stir-fries, and a variety of spicy Asian dishes such as Indian and Thai curries. Britain's rich heritage of immigration is reflected in the wide variety of ingredients available in supermarkets. Cooking, food, restaurants, food magazines, and TV shows with celebrity chefs, such as Nigella Lawson and Jamie Oliver, are popular interests.

TRADITIONAL BRITISH FOOD

The traditional British breakfast is a hearty affair, requiring a huge appetite and ample time. It is usually prepared as a weekend or holiday treat. Grilled or fried pork sausages, sliced bacon, mushrooms, tomatoes, and baked beans are served together with fried, scrambled, or poached eggs, toast, or fried or "eggy" bread. It may be accompanied by regional specialties such as lambs' kidneys; blood pudding, a type of rich sausage; oatcakes, which are like small pancakes; or fried potatoes and cabbage, known as "bubble and squeak."

Many British foods have delightful names. Here are just a few: bangers and mash (sausages and mashed potatoes); Cullen skink (smoked haddock soup); rumbledethumps (cabbage, potato, and cheese casserole); toad in the hole (sausages baked in a batter); jam roly-poly (a jam cakeroll), Eton mess (strawberries, cream, and meringue), and spotted dick (a currant-filled sponge pudding).

Everyday lunch and dinner meals are similar to those in Canada and the United States, though sometimes the dishes have different names. In Britain, the potatoes Americans know as French fries are called "chips"; while the American chips—potato chips, corn chips and the like—are "crisps." A much loved English dish is fish and chips, which is batter-fried white fish with fried potatoes.

Traditional Sunday dinner, called the Sunday Roast, is often served at lunchtime. It features a roast beef with gravy, Yorkshire pudding, which is a an eggy batter cooked in the meat's juices; potatoes; vegetables, such as carrots, peas, or turnip; and a "sweet," or dessert.

PUDDINGS AND PIES In Britain, a pudding is not what Americans call pudding. Rather, it can be a sweet or savory dish of mixed ingredients. The term "pudding" covers a wide variety of dishes, some are casserole-like, others are cake-like, and still others defy categorization. The common thread seems to be that they are homey and comforting. A sweet pudding may be a cake-like dish that is steamed or boiled. A typical example is a "figgy pudding,"

A Christmas pudding is decorated with walnuts.

or a Christmas pudding, a dark, spicy, steamed fruitcake made with breadcrumbs, sugar, raisins or other dried fruits, suet, and a bit of brandy, sherry, or rum. Summer pudding, on the other hand, is made with bread and fresh berries.

A savory pudding can be a sausage, such as a black pudding, which is a blood sausage of pork blood mixed with oatmeal; or a white pudding, a sausage of pork meat, fat, suet, and oatmeal. Preparations such as these date back several centuries.

Even a pie can be a pudding—shepherd's pie is a casserole of minced lamb (or beef), vegetables, and gravy with a mashed potato topping; steak and kidney pie is diced beef, kidneys, and gravy in a pie crust; and the amusingly named "toad in the hole," is a dish of sausages baked in a pancake-like batter.

LOCAL SPECIALTIES Scotland is well known for its salmon and river trout, as well as its beef raised on the Highland moors. The national dish of Scotland is haggis, a savory pudding made of a sheep's innards (heart, liver, and lungs), minced with onion, oatmeal, suet, and spices, which is then encased in a sheep's stomach (or a standard sausage casing) and simmered for about three hours. Tender Welsh lamb is usually served with mint sauce and vegetables. Oysters from East Anglia are a delicacy traditionally served only during months with an "r" in them.

A traditional haggis is prepared for a Burns Night Dinner in Scotland.

THE PUB

Pubs abound in Britain—there are some forty-eight thousand of them—and often play an important role in the community. Taken from the term "public house," meaning "open to the public," the pub typically serves as a place for local people to gather for a pint and some "pub grub," or homey food, discuss

A bartender works in a typical pub in London.

local events, and perhaps play some darts. Beer, ale, and hard cider are usually the preferred drinks. The legal drinking age in Great Britain is eighteen, but sixteen- and seventeen-year-olds can drink beer, wine, or cider with a meal in public if they are accompanied by an adult.

With some 1,200 different brands available, beer is a national drink, made from hops and matured in oak casks. British beers, ales, stouts, and porters are traditionally darker and bitterer than traditional US styles, and are served at room temperature. Lagers, imported from Germany, Belgium, and Denmark, are increasingly popular. Like American beer, lagers are served cold.

In the West Country, cider is brewed from apples; some rough local brews known as *scrumpy* are extremely strong. Wine is produced in Kent and Sussex in the south of England, where commercial vineyards have proved moderately successful in penetrating the local market. In general, however, most of England's climate is not suitable for growing wine grapes.

>

TEA, A DRINK AND A MEAL

The British are the largest per capita consumers of tea in the world, drinking about one-fifth of the world's total tea exports. The custom of afternoon tea, a light meal at 4 p.m. was established during the 1840s by the Duchess of Bedford. Tea is typically accompanied by small homemade cakes, scones, cookies, sandwiches, toasted muffins, or crumpets.

Whiskies from Scotland's one hundred distilleries remain a profitable export, and numerous blended whiskies, and single and double malt whiskies are matured on Scottish islands such as Jura and Islay. Gin, a spirit flavored with juniper berries, dates to the Middle Ages, and numerous brands are made in England and Scotland.

INTERNET LINKS

projectbritain.com/food/index.htm
Project Britain's site covers all areas of British life, including an in-depth section about foods and food culture.

www.historic-uk.com/CultureUK/History-of-British-Food/
Historic UK offers a "History of British Food" with links to other food related topics.

www.buzzfeed.com/jenniferschaffer/yum-british-food
"23 Classic British Dishes To Keep You Warm Through The Long, Dark Winter" on BuzzFeed has mouth-watering photos of iconic British foods.

WELSH CAKES (*PICE AR Y MAEN*)

These little cakes can be eaten out of hand for breakfast, afternoon tea, or a snack.

1 ½ cup all-purpose flour
½ cup sugar
1 tsp. baking powder
¼ tsp. nutmeg
⅛ tsp. salt
½ cup cold butter
1 large egg, beaten
¼ cup to ½ cup golden raisins or currants
¼ cup milk

Stir together flour, sugar, baking powder, nutmeg, and salt. Cut in the butter until mixture is crumbly. Add raisins or currants; add the egg and milk and mix until combined. Turn the sticky dough onto a well-floured surface and shape into a disc. Can be refrigerated at this point.

Roll or pat the dough to ¼-inch thick and cut into 2 ½-inch to 3 ½-inch rounds, adding flour underneath as needed to keep the dough from sticking. Reshape the dough scraps until used up.

Cook on a buttered griddle or in a heavy bottomed pan over low-medium heat for about three minutes per side or until they are golden brown. If they look as if they are browning too quickly, turn the heat down so they can cook through. Dust finished cakes with cinnamon-sugar or powdered sugar, or split and spread with butter and honey or jam.
Makes approximately twelve cakes.

SUMMER PUDDING

Plan ahead when making this no-bake English dessert. It needs to sit for at least eight hours, or overnight in the refrigerator.

1 cup sugar
juice of ½ lemon
6 ½ cups very ripe berries (raspberries, blackberries, strawberries, or a mix)
About 24 slices of firm-textured white bread, crusts trimmed

Line a 1-quart charlotte mold, souffle dish, or mixing bowl with plastic wrap, letting the excess hang over the sides.
Add berries and sugar to a saucepan and cook over medium heat just until sugar dissolves, about three to five minutes. Squeeze in lemon juice, stir gently and cool to lukewarm.

Cut sixteen bread slices at an angle across two opposite sides to make triangles with two long, even sides and a narrower base. Cut the remaining slices in half lengthwise to make rectangles about 3 inches (7.6 cm) long. Arrange half the bread triangles with their points to the center on the bottom of the mold or bowl to cover it completely. Arrange the rectangular slices around the sides, overlapping them slightly. Fill any gaps with scraps of bread.

Spoon half the berries and their juice into the bread-lined mold. Top with bread slices cut to fit. Add remaining berries and top with more bread, as tightly as possible. Let cool. Cover pudding with plastic wrap, place a plate on top, and weigh it down with two large cans. Place bowl on a plate (juice may seep out) and refrigerate for at least eight hours. Bread will absorb the red juices. Invert pudding onto a slightly bowled or lipped platter (to catch the juices). Remove plastic wrap and cut into wedges. Serve cold with whipped cream.

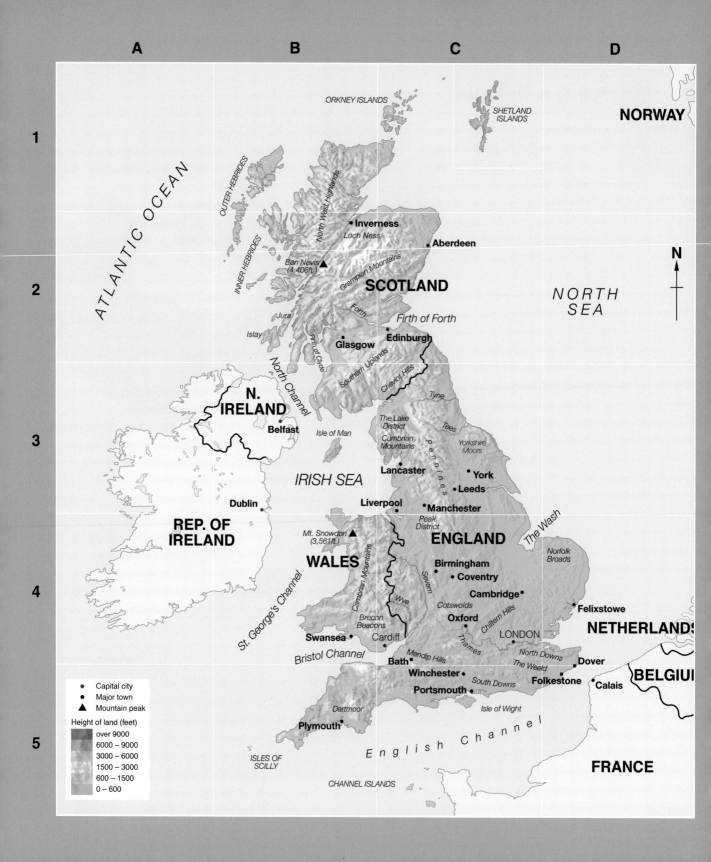

MAP OF GREAT BRITAIN

Aberdeen, C2
Atlantic Ocean,
  A1—A2

Bath, C4
Belfast, B3
Belgium, D4—D5
Ben Nevis, B2
Birmingham, C4
Brecon Beacons,
  B4—C4
Bristol Channel,
  B4

Calais, D5
Cambrian
  Mountains, B4
Cambridge, C4
Cardiff, C4
Channel Islands,
  C5
Cheviot Hills, C3
Chiltern Hills, C4
Cotswolds, C4
Coventry, C4
Cumbrian
  Mountains, C3

Dartmoor, B5
Dover, D4
Dublin, B3

Edinburgh, C2
England, C4
English Channel,
  B5—C5

Felixstowe, D4
Folkestone, D5

Firth of Clyde,
  B2—B3
Firth of Forth, C2
France, C5—D5

Glasgow, B2
Grampian
  Mountains,
  B2—C2

Inner Hebrides,
  B2
Inverness, B2
Irish Sea, B3
Islay, B2
Isle of Man, B3
Isles of Scilly, B5
Isle of Wight, C5

Jura, B2

Lake District, C3
Lancaster, C3
Leeds, C3
Liverpool, C3
Loch Ness, B2
London, C4

Manchester, C3
Mendip Hills, C4
Mount Snowdon,
  B4

Netherlands, D4
Norfolk Broads,
  D4
North Channel,
  B3
North Downs,

C4—D4
North Sea, D2
North West
  Highlands, B1—
  B2
Northern Ireland,
  B3
Norway, D1

Orkney Islands,
  C1
Outer Hebrides,
  B1
Oxford, C4

Peak District, C4
Pennines, C3
Plymouth, B5
Portsmouth, C5

Republic of
  Ireland, A3—
  B3, A4—B4
River Forth, B2
River Severn, C4
River Tees, C3
River Thames, C4
River Tyne, C3
River Wye, C4

Saint George's
  Channel, B4
Scotland, B2—C2
Shetland Islands,
  C1
South Downs, C5
Southern
  Uplands, B3, C2
Swansea, B4

Wales, B4
Wash, C4
Weald, C4—C5
Winchester, C5

York, C3
Yorkshire Moors,
  C3

133

ECONOMIC GREAT BRITAIN

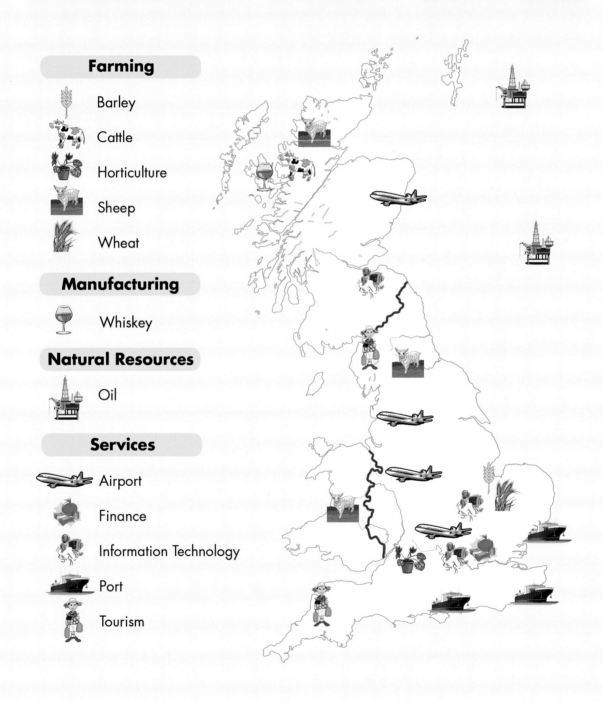

Farming
- Barley
- Cattle
- Horticulture
- Sheep
- Wheat

Manufacturing
- Whiskey

Natural Resources
- Oil

Services
- Airport
- Finance
- Information Technology
- Port
- Tourism

ABOUT THE ECONOMY

Note: Economic statistics reported here are for the entire United Kingdom.

OVERVIEW

The UK is a leading power and financial center; the third-largest economy in Europe after Germany and France. Agriculture is intensive, highly mechanized, and efficient, producing about 60 percent of food needs with less than 2 percent of the labor force. Manufacturing has declined in importance, but still accounts for 10 percent of economic output. Great Britain has large coal, natural gas, and oil resources, but these are declining, forcing Britain to import some of its energy. The global recession of 2008 hit the British economy especially hard, prompting the government to institute austerity measures through 2017.

GROSS DOMESTIC PRODUCT (GDP)

$2.4 trillion (2013)

GDP PER CAPITA

$37,300 (2013)

GDP SECTORS

Agriculture 0.7 percent, industry 20.5 percent, services 78.9 percent (2013)

INFLATION RATE

1.2 percent (September 2014)

CURRENCY

1 pound (GBP) = 100 pence
USD 1 = GBP 0.64 (November 2014)
Notes: 5, 10, 20, 50 pounds
Coins: 1, 2, 5, 10, 20, 50 pence; 1, 2 pounds

AGRICULTURAL PRODUCTS

Wheat, barley, oats, oilseed, sugar beets, potatoes, milk, poultry, fish, cattle, wool

INDUSTRIAL PRODUCTS

Machine tools, electric power, railroad equipment, shipbuilding, aircraft, motor vehicles and parts, electronics and communications equipment, metals, coal, chemicals, petroleum, paper products, food processing, textiles, clothing

EXPORTS

Manufactured goods; fuels; chemicals; food; whiskey, beer, and other beverages

IMPORTS

Manufactured goods, machinery, fuels, foodstuff, clothing

TRADE PARTNERS

Germany, China, Netherlands, US, France, Belgium, Norway

MAJOR AIRPORTS

London Heathrow, London Gatwick, Stansted, Manchester, Birmingham, Edinburgh, Aberdeen

WORKFORCE

30.1 million (2013)

UNEMPLOYMENT RATE

6.0 percent (July 2014)

CULTURAL GREAT BRITAIN

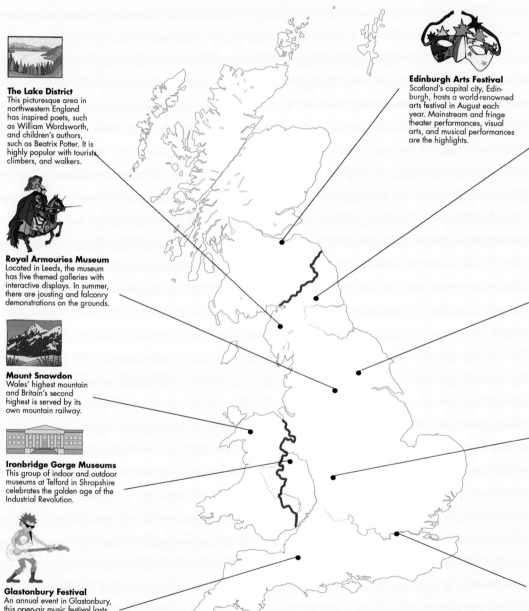

Edinburgh Arts Festival
Scotland's capital city, Edinburgh, hosts a world-renowned arts festival in August each year. Mainstream and fringe theater performances, visual arts, and musical performances are the highlights.

Hadrian's Wall
The wall was built by the Romans between A.D. 122 and 128 to keep invading Picts and Scots out of England. Many parts have been made into local farm buildings, but other parts are still recognizable today.

Jorvik Centre
The Viking days are celebrated by the Jorvik Centre in York. Residents walk dressed as Vikings, Viking-age streets are re-created, and archaeological finds are displayed.

Warwick Castle
A major center of power in medieval times, the castle in Warwickshire is very well-preserved, and a visit to its high battlements and furnished rooms gives real insight into former days.

London
Britain's capital city is a center of museums and is home to Westminster Abbey, the Tower of London, numerous theaters, cinemas, concert venues, and galleries.

The Lake District
This picturesque area in northwestern England has inspired poets, such as William Wordsworth, and children's authors, such as Beatrix Potter. It is highly popular with tourists, climbers, and walkers.

Royal Armouries Museum
Located in Leeds, the museum has five themed galleries with interactive displays. In summer, there are jousting and falconry demonstrations on the grounds.

Mount Snowdon
Wales' highest mountain and Britain's second highest is served by its own mountain railway.

Ironbridge Gorge Museums
This group of indoor and outdoor museums at Telford in Shropshire celebrates the golden age of the Industrial Revolution.

Glastonbury Festival
An annual event in Glastonbury, this open-air music festival lasts three days in June and features rock band performances, fringe theater shows, and circus and cabaret acts.

ABOUT THE CULTURE

OFFICIAL NAME
Great Britain is the largest of the 2,000 or so islands that make up the British Isles.

NATIONAL FLAG
England, Scotland, and Wales each has its own flag. The United Kingdom flag, known as the Union Jack, consists of England's red cross of its patron saint, Saint George, on a white background, combined with Scotland's diagonal white cross of its patron saint, Saint Andrew, on a blue background and Ireland's red diagonal cross of Saint Patrick. The flag of Wales, a red dragon on a green and white background, is not integrated into the Union design.

CAPITALS
UK and England—London
Wales—Cardiff (Caerdydd)
Scotland—Edinburgh

POPULATION
61.9 million (2014)

LITERACY RATE
99 percent

LIFE EXPECTANCY AT BIRTH
80.4 years; 78.3 years for men, 82.7 years for women (2014)

NATIONAL HOLIDAYS
New Year's Day (January 1), Good Friday and Easter Monday (March/April), Early May Holiday (Monday nearest May 1), Spring Bank Holiday (Monday at end of May, formerly Whitsun), Summer Bank Holiday (last Monday in August), Christmas Day and Boxing Day (December 25 and 26)

ETHNIC GROUPS
White 87.2 percent, black/African/Caribbean 3 percent, Asian/Asian British: Indian 2.3 percent; Pakistani 1.9 percent, mixed 2 percent; other 3.7 percent (2011)

RELIGIONS
Christian 59.5 percent, Muslim 4.4 percent, Hindu 1.3 percent, other 2 percent, none 25.7 percent, unspecified 7.2 percent (2011)

LANGUAGES
English, Scots, Scottish Gaelic, Welsh, Cornish

LEADERS IN POLITICS
Tony Blair, UK prime minister (1997—2007)
Gordon Brown, prime minister (2007—2010)
David Cameron, prime minister (2010—)
Alex Salmond, first minister of Scotland (2007—2014)
Carwyn Jones, first minister of Wales (2009—)

TIMELINE

IN GREAT BRITAIN	IN THE WORLD

6500 BCE
English Channel formed
4000–1500 BCE
Henges, including Stonehenge, constructed

753 BCE
Rome is founded.

43 CE
Aulus Plautius invades Britain.

116–117 CE
The Roman Empire reaches its greatest extent,
under Emperor Trajan (reigned 98–117 CE).

122–128
Hadrian's Wall constructed
410
Romans leave Britain
597
Saint Augustine and forty monks arrive
from Rome
871
King Ethelred and his brother, the future
King Alfred the Great, defeat the Danes.

600 CE
Height of Mayan civilization

1337
Start of Hundred Years' War
1348
Start of Black Death
1536
Act of Union joins Wales to England.

1000
The Chinese perfect gunpowder and
begin to use it in warfare.

1530
Beginning of transAtlantic slave trade organized
by the Portuguese in Africa.
1558–1603
Reign of Elizabeth I of England
1620
Pilgrims sail the *Mayflower* to America.

1588
The Spanish Armada is defeated.
1642–1651
English Civil War
1666
Great Fire of London
1707
Act of Union joins Scotland to England.
1775–1783
American War of Independence

1776
US Declaration of Independence written
1789–1799
The French Revolution

IN GREAT BRITAIN	IN THE WORLD
1793–1815 Britain goes to war against France in the Napoleonic Wars.	
1857 Indian Mutiny, a rebellion against British rule in India	**1861** The US Civil War begins.
1870 Education Act established, becomes foundation for modern education system	**1869** The Suez Canal is opened.
1922 BBC, then known as the British Broadcasting Company, established	**1914** World War I begins.
1947 India and Pakistan gain independence.	**1939** World War II begins.
	1949 The North Atlantic Treaty Organization (NATO) is formed.
1956 Crisis over control of Suez Canal involving Britain, France, and the Middle East	**1957** The Russians launch *Sputnik*.
	1966–1969 The Chinese Cultural Revolution
1982 Falklands War between Argentina and Britain	**1986** Nuclear power disaster at Chernobyl in Ukraine
	1991 Breakup of the Soviet Union
1997 Tony Blair becomes prime minister; Diana, Princess of Wales, dies	**1997** Britain returns Hong Kong to China.
	2001 Terrorists crash planes in New York, Washington, DC, and Pennsylvania.
2005 Suicide bombers kill fifty-two people on London's transport system	**2003** War in Iraq begins.
	2008 US elects first African American president, Barack Obama.
2014 Scotland votes to remain a part of the United Kingdom	**2014** Ebola epidemic in West Africa kills more than five thousand people.

GLOSSARY

ale
A bitter beer made from rapid fermentation of malt, hops, and yeast at a high temperature.

barrow
A communal burial ground in southern England.

Caledonia
An old name for Scotland.

constitutional monarchy
A political system that legally limits the actions of the king or queen.

devolution
The delegation of certain powers by a central authority to regional governments.

Druids
An ancient order of Celts consisting of learned men who were usually judges, priests, or teachers.

eisteddfod (aye-STED-fod)
A poetry, singing, and musical competition during which all proceedings are held in Welsh.

Gaelic
The Celtic language of Scotland.

glen
A narrow, secluded valley.

Huguenots
Protestants in France in the sixteenth and seventeenth centuries.

loch (LOCK)
The Scottish term for a deep lake.

Magna Carta
A historical document that guaranteed political rights and personal liberties in Britain.

operetta
A comical or romantic opera.

peers
Members of the House of Lords, Britain's upper house of Parliament.

ria (REE-ah)
A coast characterized by a series of long, narrow, wedge-shaped inlets that widen and deepen uniformly toward the sea.

tartan
A fabric of Scottish origin that has a plaid design and is traditionally made into a kilt.

tor
A high, craggy hill.

weald
A forest or wooded area.

Witan
An Anglo-Saxon council of men that decided on royal succession and other policy matters.

FOR FURTHER INFORMATION

BOOKS

Banker, Leslie, and William Mullins. *Britannia in Brief: The Scoop on All Things British*. New York: Ballantine Books/Random House, Inc., 2009.

DK Eyewitness Travel Guide: Great Britain. New York: DK Publishing, 2014.

Fraser, Rebecca. *The Story of Britain: From the Romans to the Present*. New York: W. W. Norton & Co., 2005.

Fry, Plantagenet Somerset. *Kings & Queens of England and Scotland*. New York: DK Adult, 2011.

History of Britain and Ireland. New York: DK Publishing, 2011.

Lacey, Robert. *Great Tales from English History: A Treasury of True Stories about the Extraordinary People—Knights and Knaves, Rebels and Heroes, Queens and Commoners—Who Made Britain Great*. New York: Back Bay Books/Little, Brown and Company, 2007.

FILM

A History of Scotland (a ten-part series). BBC Home Entertainment, 2010. DVD.

Anne of the Thousand Days. Universal Studios, 1969. DVD.

Brave. Disney-Pixar, 2012. DVD.

Michael Wood's Story of England. BBC Home Entertainment, 2012. DVD.

The Madness of King George. MGM, 1996. DVD.

The Queen. Miramax Lionsgate, 2006. DVD or Blu-ray.

The Story of Wales. Bfs Entertainment, 2012. DVD.

WEBSITES

BBC Goodfood, British recipes. www.bbcgoodfood.com/recipes/collection/british

Britain Is Great. www.gov.uk/britainisgreat

Britannia. www.britannia.com

British Broadcasting Corporation. www.bbc.com

British Monarchy. www.royal.gov.uk

Britroyals. www.britroyals.com/timeline.asp

Environment Agency. www.gov.uk/government/organisations/environment-agency

Gov.UK. www.gov.uk

VisitBritain. www.visitbritain.com/en/US

VisitScotland. www.visitscotland.com/en-us

Wales Cymru. www.visitwales.com

BIBLIOGRAPHY

BOOKS AND WEBSITES

Al Jazeera.com, "Poll: Muhammad most popular boy's name in UK," Al Jazeera, Dec. 1, 2014 www.aljazeera.com/news/europe/2014/12/mohamed-now-uk-now-most-popular-boys-name-2014121112154850319.html

BBC News Europe. "United Kingdom Profile." www.bbc.com/news/world-europe-18023389

British Monarchy. www.royal.gov.uk

Bryson, Bill. *The Mother Tongue: English & How It Got That Way*. New York: William Morrow & Co., 1990.

Carrington, Damian. "Climate change will make UK weather too wet and too dry, says Met Office." *The Guardian*, March 25, 2014. www.theguardian.com/environment/2014/mar/25/climate-change-uk-weather-wet-dry-met-office

Cook, Sonia Van Gilder. "First Come, First Crowned: The British Monarchy Gets Modern." *Time*, Oct. 31, 2011. content.time.com/time/world/article/0,8599,2098162,00.html

Dugan, Emily. "Teenage pregnancies in England and Wales are at the lowest point since records began." *The Independent*, Feb. 25, 2014. www.independent.co.uk/life-style/Hui, Sylvia. "In UK, aristocrats still face 'Downton' dilemma." AP The Big Story, April 12, 2013. bigstory.ap.org/article/uk-aristocrats-still-face-downton-dilemma

Jones, Jonathan. "Blake's heaven." *The Guardian*, April 25, 2005. www.theguardian.com/culture/2005/apr/25/williamblake

Legatum Institute. "Legatum Prosperity Index 2014." www.prosperity.com

Martin, Arthur. "How 94% of fish stocks have vanished from British waters." *The Daily Mail*, May 5, 2010. www.dailymail.co.uk/news/article-1272378/Extraordinary-decline-British-fish-stocks-drop-94-cent.html

Matthews, John. *King Arthur, Dark Age Warrior and Mythic Hero*. London: Carlton Books, 2004.

Mount, Harry. "Queen Elizabeth II: the most dutiful monarch in a thousand years." *The Telegraph*, March 13, 2013. www.telegraph.co.uk/news/uknews/

Office for National Statistics. "2011 Census for England and Wales." www.ons.gov.uk/ons/guide-method/census/2011/index.html

United Kingdom Government. www.gov.uk

Urquhart, Conal. "Flooding and storms in UK are clear signs of climate change, says Lord Stern." *The Guardian*, Feb. 13, 2014. www.theguardian.com/environment/2014/feb/13/flooding-storms-uk-climate-change-lord-stern?CMP=EMCNEWEML6619I2

Wintour, Patrick. "David Cameron: UK may be a small island but it has the biggest heart." *The Guardian*, Sept. 6, 2013. www.theguardian.com/politics/2013/sep/06/david-cameron-uk-small-island

INDEX

INDEX